Beautifully Broken

Finding Hope During Loss

PAT ELSBERRY

Praise for
Beautifully Broken: Finding Hope During Loss

"Words mean a lot to me, they represent emotion, beauty, and ideas. Sentences help marry my heart and mind in a ceremony of grace and truth. My friend Pat in *Beautifully Broken* has done a remarkable job prayerfully weaving words into sentences, seamlessly together in a way that invited me into her love story. She has accomplished the difficult task of making Jesus the hero throughout the incredible challenges of loving her daughter well within horrific circumstances. It's at this life crossroads of giving up or holding on to trust in God that Pat kept her faith. I pray and believe this book will help many, many families find hope, forgiveness, love, and peace through *Beautifully Broken*. And most of all, celebrate how Pat found joy in her pain, through the love of her Lord and Savior Jesus Christ."

—Boyd Bailey
Wisdom Hunters

"For anyone experiencing the painful realities of a loved one battling substance addictions, *Beautifully Broken* offers "from the trenches" insights from one that has been there. Pat Elsberry bravely shares, with poignance and candor, her family's personal journey with a child battling Substance Use Disorder (SUD). Most importantly, she shares intimate perspectives for healing and hope as she walks the grief journey."

—William F. "Woody" Faulk
Vice President, Innovation and New Ventures
Chick-fil-A, Inc.

"Pat Elsberry, in her book *Beautifully Broken: Finding Hope During Loss*, shares her riveting story with grief, loss, and hope! This book is a must read for those who have experienced tragedy and are looking for perspective. Pat's story is one that many can relate to and a place to find hope and healing. If you have lost someone to addiction and are looking for comfort this book is for you!"

—Pastor Jeremy Usry
Campus Pastor
Church of the King

"Being invited into Pat's *Beautifully Broken* journey has been such an honor. The unique privilege of sitting with her and hearing her heart has been a source of inspiration for me. This brokenhearted mother's devotion and long-suffering through her Melanie's difficult years of Substance Use Disorder are so adeptly expressed in this book. Having counseled with countless grieving parents over the past 35 years, this book will definitely be a healing resource which I would highly recommend. Pat shows the many ups and downs of this arduous road. However, she does not "*sorrow as those who have no hope*" *(I Thes 4:13)*. Pat excellently shares the comforting work of our Lord in her recovery. You will be encouraged by her vulnerable communication."

—Gretchen Peacock
Doctor of Marital and Family Therapy,
Licensed Professional Counselor

"Pat Elsberry gives us the rare opportunity to express our spiritual woundedness. She invites us to weep, to remember, to feel, and yes, to heal. Embrace this book. Or better yet, let the love and hope of this book embrace you."

—Cheryl Juaire
President/Founder of the National Grief
Support Organization, Team Sharing

"*Beautifully Broken* is a mother's heartfelt, and often painful journey through her daughter's long battle with the disease of addiction. It is also a shining light on dealing with grief and finding hope during loss. Propelled by her own devastation, Pat shares the emotional rollercoaster of highs and lows as she brings to the forefront, an often-ignored truth: that drug addiction is not a choice. It is a courageous telling of a story fraught with trials, from one who knows, that ultimately, Jesus Christ makes all things good. The result is an ongoing mission to eliminate the stigma of drug addiction and expose it for what it really is: a disease. This book is highly recommended to anyone who needs to find hope and comfort while walking their grief journey, as the words of wisdom are from one who has experienced it firsthand."

—Joyce DeSanctis
Friend

"*Beautifully Broken* is a great read! By using a conversational style of writing, Pat Elsberry welcomes the reader into an intimate conversation about one of the most painful things imaginable – the death of one's child. In this poignant story she shares intimate details of her arduous journey through the valley of the shadow of death. All along the way Pat talks with the reader and continuously reminds them that Jesus, the strength of her life, is the reason for her getting to the other side of "through." It is a book of urgent need particularly for those suffering through the turmoil of our nation's current plague of children with Substance Use Disorder (SUD). Pat provides the hurting a safe passage through that lonesome valley with the comforting love of Jesus as her guide.

—Rowan Bronson, Ed. D.
Friend

"Although I have known Pat Elsberry and her daughter Melanie, for over 30 years I was not aware of the impact Substance Use Disorder could have in someone's life. This transparent and vulnerable retelling of the early years, ultimately ending in Melanie's untimely death, has once again gripped my heart. Even knowing many of these stories, until I read *Beautifully Broken* I didn't realize the depth of Pat's sorrow and pain. During her grief journey Pat has truly taken off "her mask" and let her guard down for all the world to see.

As a fellow believer, I am greatly encouraged by the love that God has shown to Pat, every step of the way. God doesn't promise us that He will remove our pain & sorrow, after all we are not in heaven yet, but clearly He has made a way for Pat to grieve well. I have no doubt that this mother's grief journey will reach untold others who are struggling with the loss of their loved one. Whether it is the death of a child, a spouse, a friend, etc., grief is grief, and death is a part of life that none of us is exempt from dealing with. Please allow Pat's unfolding of this story of love and loss bring light into your darkness."

—Kathleen McLendon
Friend

Beautifully Broken

Finding Hope During Loss

Ordering Information:
For details, contact www.hopeduringloss.com

This memoir is a truthful recollection of actual events in the author's life. The events, places, and conversations in this memoir have been recreated from memory. Some conversations have been recreated and/or supplemented. The chronology of some events has been compressed. When necessary, the names and identifying characteristics of individuals and places have been changed to maintain anonymity.

Print ISBN: 978-1-66780-919-9
eBook ISBN: 978-1-66780-920-5

Printed in the United States of America on SFI Certified paper.

First Edition

Dedicated with love to Melanie Anne Travassos

(Mel-Mel, forever my girl)

CONTENTS

PROLOGUE

It had never occurred to me that I'd be writing a book about the death of my only daughter, Melanie, or the disease of addiction that stole her from my life. Although I had dreamed about writing a book one day, I certainly didn't expect it to be on this subject. However, like many others before me, I found myself thrust into a world I never anticipated being a part of and becoming a member of a group no parent would ask to join. Yet here I am.

Melanie had many periods of sobriety, along with multiple rehab opportunities, but ultimately the disease of Substance Use Disorder (SUD) claimed her life here on earth. After 18 months of sobriety, on February 19, 2020 my beautiful girl was found dead in a hotel room as the result of an accidental drug overdose.

As the mom of a child who suffered from SUD I always knew this could happen but it's something you hope never becomes a reality. It's the call you expect but hope to never receive. Parents should not outlive their children. Death is hard, and an out-of-order death is not a journey I would wish upon anyone. Although my heart has been broken in ways that are oftentimes indescribable, I have also experienced a peace that truly has surpassed all understanding. This peace comes from my Lord and Savior, Jesus Christ. If it weren't for him, I wouldn't be able to get up each day. And even on those days that are still raw, it's my faith that sustains me and lifts me up.

1

One day while Melanie was in rehab she called me on the phone. "Mom I had to write a poem for one of my classes and today I had the chance to share it with everyone. I was so nervous but after I finished everyone stood up and gave me a standing ovation. They loved it, and I want to read it to you, Mom." I could hear the pride in her voice as she spoke, and as she began to read the words I was brought to tears because it was the essence of who she was – my beautifully broken girl.

I Am
I am broken but beautifully made
I wonder if I'll make it after this
I hear my son's voice
I see myself walking out of these gates
I want to be sober for the rest of my life
I am broken but beautifully made

I pretend like I have it all together
I feel like crying
I touch my chest because my heart is broken
I worry that I will fail and not succeed
I cry when I feel alone
I am broken but beautifully made

I understand I am stuck with this disease
I say have faith, this too shall pass
I dream about being in better places soon
I try to please those that don't care about me
I hope to be happy with who I've become
I am broken but beautifully made

When I read this now my heart simultaneously breaks and soars. She was sometimes complex, yet simple and carefree as well. It was like dealing with two different people. There was kind, easy-going, happy, lighthearted Melanie and then there was the total opposite - sad, depressed, angry, emotional, unreasonable Melanie who would have outbursts at any given moment. She was in such conflict with herself, but that is what happens when you have SUD. It wasn't who she wanted to be. While in recovery she had an opportunity to view herself with a different set of eyes. She realized she was beautiful, inside, and out, yet due to the disease of addiction and all she had lost as a result of it, she was also broken. If only she had realized, we cannot get through life without enduring some type of loss along life's journey. Somewhere within each of us, we are all beautiful but broken.

While giving Melanie's eulogy I spoke about her heart. I wanted to encourage those who had attended and were still actively walking in their addiction, as well as the others who were sober and working their program. I wanted them to hear about Melanie's heart. Her true heart. Not the heart of the person with SUD, but the heart of the girl who still loved Jesus even though she struggled with the disease of addiction. My girl is walking streets of gold, no longer struggling with the daily pull of getting high. She's at peace, and happy. Walking and talking with her Heavenly Father.

I don't claim to have all the answers, but what I do know is this - it doesn't really matter what your loved one died of. Whether it was the disease of addiction, cancer, suicide, car accident, or miscarriage – loss is loss and grief is grief. All of our hearts break the same, regardless of the reason. I hope walking along this journey with me, whatever your struggle may be, will encourage you to reach for the one who *"heals the brokenhearted and saves those who are crushed in spirit." (Psalm 34:18)*

My heart's desire is that as I share our journey with you, your own heart will be deeply touched in ways you never imagined. For in the end, I believe God's abundant grace, comfort and mercy will be revealed.

Part One:
Life's Journey:
How We Got Here

For I know the plans I have for you," declares the LORD,
*"plans to prosper you and not to harm you, plans
to give you hope and a future" Jeremiah 29:11*

Melanie's Life Scripture

CHAPTER 1

The Encounter

When I woke up on February 18, 2020, I had an uneasiness deep within me. We were scheduled to travel to Naples, Florida that afternoon for a much-anticipated winter break. It had been raining for weeks and I couldn't wait to feel the sunshine on my face and the sand between my toes. As much as I had looked forward to this vacation, I received some news a few days before that was like a sucker punch to the gut. My daughter, Melanie, who struggled with the disease of Substance Use Disorder (SUD) had relapsed after being clean and sober for 18 months. While this was devastating news, I was also weary from all the ups and downs of dealing with the aftermath the disease of addiction can bring. I just wanted to put it aside for a few days of peace and quiet in the Florida sunshine.

I hit the ground running early as I took care of some last-minute work issues. While finalizing our packing, I realized I would need to make a quick run to Target after my shower to pick up a few things before heading to the airport. By this time, I had tucked away any uneasiness I felt in that secret place, where I had long ago learned to hide things in order to survive being the mom of a child with the disease of addiction. I focused on the tasks at hand, doing what needed to be done to stay on track.

At 9:45 a.m. I turned on the shower letting it get hot and steamy. Our shower is enclosed in glass and when I saw the steam billowing out from above that was my queue it was ready. A moment after I stepped in, I turned and looked outward into the bathroom when in front of me I saw my father – my father who had died 42 years ago! I looked at him, and quickly began assessing what was before me. He looked so much younger than I had remembered him to be, and his eyes though looking toward me did not appear to look directly at me. In hindsight, this made me feel better since I am, after all, in the shower. I literally closed my eyes, squeezing them tightly shut and re-opening them. When I did, he was still there. He was dressed completely in white, wearing a long-sleeve, white button-down shirt with a stand-up collar. The buttons were brown and were very small unlike what you would see on a shirt today. As my eyes began to follow his body downward, I didn't see pants or legs but only what appeared to me as a very thick, heavy white coat. In this moment, I assumed I wasn't seeing his legs because of the substantial steam covering the shower door.

All of this took place in a matter of seconds. After blinking my eyes, it didn't take long for the reality of what I was seeing to hit me and when it did, I became filled with fear. I had once heard that when people are dying, many times their loved ones who have gone to heaven before them appear, to escort them home. Is this what was happening? Was I getting ready to die?

I immediately turned my back to him facing the corner of the shower and began to fervently pray. Any scripture I could think of that filled my mind came out of my mouth: "No weapon formed against me will prosper." "I will live and not die and declare the works of the Lord." "I bind you Satan in Jesus name. You will not have me." After standing there praying for I don't know how long, I opened my eyes and simply began showering. I've reflected back on this many times and not only did any fear I previously felt leave me, in fact I actually felt nothing at all. It was as if what I just witnessed never happened.

If that sounds unbelievable, I understand. It's pretty incredulous to me, too. It's not that I simply put what happened aside and didn't *want* to think about it –it was as if it had been wiped from my memory. This encounter with my father was not brought back to my remembrance until 42 hours later. But I don't want to get ahead of my story.

If you haven't put this book down yet or had a moment's thought that I'm crazy, you're probably not human. Just joking - well, maybe only a bit. Nothing like this has ever happened to me before and I truly doubt it will ever happen again. I also seriously questioned if telling this part of my story was the right thing to do. However, I believe if I didn't reveal this, I would have missed out on sharing one of the most profound parts of my story and that is, how God allows the most unbelievable things to happen because there will be no denying that he alone is the one who allowed it to be. As with most stories, before we can move forward, we need to go back for a moment. Here is where my story really begins.

Moment of Reflection: Has something seemingly unbelievable ever happened to you? What did you do?

CHAPTER 2

The Early Days of Marriage

When I was barely 18 years old I married my childhood sweetheart, Justin. We grew up together and started dating at a young age. He was one of the popular kids and had natural athletic ability, lettering in several sports. I was quiet, loved school, cooking with my mom, going to the Friday night church dances, and hanging out with my girlfriends. As different as we were, we loved one another - whatever love means when you're a teenager! Soon after graduating from high school I found myself pregnant. Unfortunately, only a few weeks after sharing this news with my parents my father got in a car accident and was killed instantly. He was only 58 years old. It was a life changer for me and the first traumatic thing I had ever experienced in my young life. Nonetheless, my mom was adamant about me getting married and made it clear this was not open for negotiation. So, instead of going off to college as I had planned, we went off to City Hall to get married.

The early days of our marriage were like most newlyweds. We were young, happy, and very naive! Soon after having our first child, a beautiful little boy named John, the reality and responsibility of life set in. Justin had the lethal combination of severe anger issues, along with an addiction problem. Back in those days most would not have considered him an addict at all, but just another young guy experimenting and partying like all the guys his age. He was what most would consider a "functioning addict." Unfortunately for me the worst part about this was when he was high, he was abusive. During those days battered women's syndrome was not openly discussed. As a matter of fact, you weren't supposed to talk about it at all and I was made to think I was the cause of his explosive temper and beatings. I was told, "surely there must be something you're doing to set him off? You made your bed and now you need to lie in it!"

About 2 ½ years into our marriage I was pregnant with our second child. Over Labor Day we went on a picnic to one of the local state parks with a group of friends. While I cared for our son, Justin was off drinking and partying. We had driven to the state park with another couple and when we arrived back in the city to pick up our car, I hopped into the driver's seat to make our way home. Justin began yelling and screaming at me insisting he was going to drive. Unfortunately, I felt I had no choice but to give in and let him take the wheel in his inebriated condition. During the drive he began shouting and telling me how I had embarrassed him in front of our friends, while he repeatedly punched me in the head and the side of my face.

Instead of going home he pulled up in front of a local park where many of our friends were hanging out. As soon as the car stopped, I jumped out and got our little boy from the back seat. All I could think of was that I needed to get away from him. My best friend, Patty, lived up the street and I knew if I could just get there, I would be safe. The moment I started running away with my little boy in my arms, Justin was at my side. He began pulling our son from me like a rag doll, with me holding one half of him while he pulled the other. I immediately let go so he wouldn't get ripped in half but the moment I did Justin began pummeling me in my abdomen and chest. I was able to get away and ran to Patty's house where we called the police.

Once the police arrived, they escorted me to the park to get my son and speak with my husband. The moment Justin saw me walk in with the police by my side he immediately went into attack mode. As things began to unravel and get out of control, I found my little boy in the back seat of our car and got ourselves out of there. Although I didn't witness it, I later heard that my husband attacked the policeman and was subsequently beaten and subdued by multiple law enforcement officers. He ended up spending a few days in jail and while he was there, I packed up our things, got on a plane and flew to the safety of my sister's home in Jacksonville, Florida.

Due to the beating I received, I began exhibiting signs of a miscarriage. Once I got to Florida, I saw a doctor and thankfully the symptoms stopped, and I was able to continue with my pregnancy.

This was something that would haunt me for many years. Right up until Melanie's death I always wondered if that last beating when I almost miscarried had caused some type of brain damage to my girl. Is that why she suffered from SUD? Is that why she struggled in school? Of course, hindsight is 20/20 and I have often wondered if there was something else I could have done to stop the abuse before it got to this point. All questions I will never have an answer to this side of heaven, but it will forever haunt me.

Moment of Reflection: Have you ever found yourself running through the "what if" scenarios? What if you had made a different decision, would things have turned out differently? List some of the scenarios that play on repeat in your head.

CHAPTER 3

The God of Love or Fear?

Growing up in Cambridge, Massachusetts I was the baby of the family. My two siblings, a brother and a sister, were both much older than me. When I was 16 years old my sister came to visit one day and began telling me about Jesus. I'm not sure I ever heard anyone talk about Jesus much except for the baby who lay in a manger at Christmas. She began to share with me about how God sacrificed his only son, Jesus, on the cross so that we could have eternal life. She told me I could have a personal relationship with him, which was so different from anything I'd ever heard before.

As a young child, in my mind God was a very big, very scary guy high up in the sky. He had long hair, with blood dripping from his hands – this depiction is thanks to my mom because of all the statues she kept of him throughout the house. I also thought he was the one who waited for me to do something wrong and when I did, he would punish me. Between the statues and what I'd been told, my picture of God didn't depict love or comfort, it only created fear. I remember never wanting to look at one particular statue because the eyes seemed to follow me all around the room. Creepy!

When I was growing up we attended church every week, although I don't remember hearing much about the love of Jesus, only about all the things that would happen to me if I did something wrong. So, when my sister began talking about Jesus and how much he loved us, I became curious and wanted to know more about him. As the months went on, every time she would visit we would have many conversations about him. One Sunday I went to church with her and gave my life to the Lord. I asked Jesus to forgive me for my sins and asked him to come live in my heart and be my Lord and Savior.

Although this was a turning point in my life it would still be a few years before I would really seek after him with my whole heart and begin to live my life for him. This is also one of the most amazing things about the Christian faith. While we may not always be doing the right thing and walking the right path, he still loves us. *"But God demonstrates his own love for us in this: While we were still sinners, Christ died for us" (Romans 5:8 NIV)*. How grateful I am he never gave up on me or left me when I veered down a wrong path.

There were so many times during my abusive marriage that God intervened in my life, and I knew it was because of his great love for me that he saved me from being severely harmed. Even though it would eventually take many years to heal from the trauma of being abused, I've never once regretted giving my life to Jesus and placing my heart and trust in him.

While living in Jacksonville and contemplating what my next steps would be, my faith continued to grow stronger. I was also so thankful to be in a safe place.

With the passage of time, my husband and I began communicating and he begged me to come back home and try to piece our lives back together. He promised he would never lay another hand on me, and with one young child and another on the way I thought I should at least try one more time. Although I wasn't ready to jump all the way into the deep end and live with him, I was willing to return to Boston to give our marriage another try. In the meantime, my mother agreed to let me, and the children stay with her for a while. Interestingly, after my return to Boston, there never seemed to be a time where I felt a peace in my heart about moving back in together, so the kids and I remained living with my mother.

Moment of Reflection: Has there been a time when God rescued you? Think about a time you prayed about something, but the answer was not immediate. Did you think God didn't hear you? Did you give up? When you thought all was lost and then He showed up, what did you learn?

CHAPTER 4

Trust: Making the Path Clear

While this may seem like a somewhat unconventional arrangement, I continued to pray about what direction I was supposed to take in my marriage and continued trusting Jesus to make the way clear.

A couple of months after returning from Jacksonville as I was washing the car in the driveway my water broke. It was a beautiful, sunny day in April when Melanie decided this would be her birthday. The only thing missing was her father – he was nowhere to be found.

I got a ride to the hospital and shockingly I was the only person having a baby that day, so I had a lot of attention. I remember sitting in the rocking chair, rocking back and forth while I chatted on the phone with my mom, and watched Denny Terrio on Dance Fever. A couple of hours into labor one of the nurses appeared with my husband trailing behind her. He came stumbling in, reeking of alcohol. I refused to let him stay and after a colorful conversation, the medical staff escorted him out.

Only 5 hours after arriving at the hospital Melanie made her entrance into this world. I can still clearly see her beautiful head of dark hair and button nose as they placed her in my arms. When they did I immediately laid my hands on her, praying over her in those first few moments of her sweet life. I think somewhere within me I knew then that soon it would be just me, John, and Melanie – the 3 Musketeers.

Our lives continued to move forward but with no real direction regarding the state of my marriage. The children and I continued living with my mom in a very small, cramped one-bedroom apartment.

One day in the late Fall I began experiencing pains in my chest with every breath I took. I ended up going to the hospital and was diagnosed with a spontaneous pneumothorax - a collapsed lung. At the time, I weighed 90 lbs. soaking wet, smoked 2 packs of Marlboros a day and was stressed beyond measure. After being in the hospital for 2 weeks I was finally able to go home, avoiding surgery, at least for the time being. The apartment we lived in was a 3rd floor walk-up and when I was released from the hospital my doctor instructed me to avoid stress at all costs and to limit going up and down the 3 flights of stairs.

One morning soon after going home and while still recovering, I was awakened by the sound of the doorbell at 1:00 a.m. When I opened the door, Justin was standing there a bloodied, battered mess. He had gotten into a fight with someone and needed to go to the hospital. So, even though I knew I shouldn't go, compassion won, and I took him!

While I waited in the ER for him to be treated I once again began praying about the state of my life and marriage. *"Lord, what am I doing? What do you want for me in this life? I have two beautiful babies but since I returned from Jacksonville there are barriers at every turn when I try to put my marriage back together. This is not how I want to live. Please help me."*

After a couple of hours, we returned to my mother's apartment where we both fell asleep. Not long after, Melanie woke up to be fed and as I picked her up to place her in the highchair, I fell back as a pressure, much like a ton of bricks hit me square in the chest. Suddenly, I had a hard time breathing and felt the familiar thumping in my chest. My lung had collapsed. Again!

I managed to get myself into the bedroom to wake up Justin and tell him we needed to go back to the hospital. His response? Anger. Yelling. Cursing.

Well, he did take me, however, when we pulled up to the Emergency Room, he opened the door and told me to get out. He wasn't staying with me. I can't remember a moment in my young life when I felt more frightened or alone.

As I reflect back on that morning now, we are never truly alone. I imagine my Heavenly Father threw his arm around me and walked with me through those doors. He never left my side for one moment. *"When you go through deep waters and great trouble, I will be with you. When you go through rivers of difficulty, you will not drown! When you walk through the fire of oppression, you will not be burned up—the flames will not consume you" (Isaiah 43:2 TLB)*

Ultimately I ended up having surgery and soon after returning home I remember sitting up in bed praying: *"Jesus, I'm at the end of my rope here. I'm so unhappy and I don't know what to do about my marriage anymore. I keep hitting a roadblock at every turn. I need you to let me know beyond a shadow of a doubt if I should move forward with divorce and return to Jacksonville to start a new life, or if I should stay in this marriage and raise our family here in Boston. Lord, if you get us an apartment to live in together by January 1st, then I'll know you want me to stay. If not, I know you'll want me to move forward with the divorce and move to Florida."*

Although I wasn't intentionally testing God, I needed a sign from him. In the Old Testament in Judges 6, Gideon prays a type of prayer known as a fleece. He wanted to be sure it was really God's voice he was hearing and that he understood his direction. He asked God for a sign to prove this was truly his will. So, he left a fleece of wool outside overnight and asked God to make it wet while keeping the surrounding dirt dry. God graciously did as Gideon asked, and in the morning the fleece was wet enough to produce a bowl of water when it was wrung out. As crazy as my fleece was, I believe God knew my heart was sincere. Once I prayed that prayer, I never thought about it again, until the early morning hours of January 1st.

As my eyes began to flutter open on that New Year's morning the Holy Spirit immediately brought to my remembrance the prayer I prayed laying in that bed just 6 weeks earlier. Well, I didn't have an apartment, and in fact, had hardly seen my husband over the holidays. I instantly knew in my heart I had my answer. I would move forward with getting a divorce, and I would move back to Jacksonville to start a new life with John and Melanie.

Moment of Reflection: Have you ever tested the Lord with a fleece? I'm not sure I'd recommend it as a regular mode of prayer, but God knows the heart's intent. He knows what we need before we utter a word.

CHAPTER 5

The Three Musketeers

From the time Melanie was born there was a distinct difference between the way her father treated her and how he treated her brother, John. I didn't understand it. Shouldn't a father love both of his children? What had a young, innocent little girl ever done to him except be born?

While we lived in Jacksonville my ex-husband continued his destructive path of drinking, drugs, and abuse which resulted in John and Melanie having minimal contact with him. They would later refer to him as "Bio Dad" and as they grew older would begin calling him by his first name, as they felt he didn't deserve the title of Dad in any form. It was a very fragmented relationship, but like most children, more than anything in the world, inwardly they longed for a relationship with their father. Throughout the years there would be brief touchpoints but most of the time there was no follow-through on his behalf.

John and Melanie were born exactly 3 years and one month apart. When John's birthday would roll around a boatload of gifts would appear on the doorstep. Melanie knew her birthday was next, and she waited with childlike anticipation and excitement to see what the mailman would bring for her birthday. Sadly, the gifts never came. Instead of it being a time of fun and joy it became hurtful for both. Melanie was devastated by the abject rejection, and

John felt guilty about getting so many gifts when his little sister received nothing. The hurt inflicted upon her by her biological father was deep and after this happened several years in a row, I told him that if he couldn't send gifts to both children, he could no longer send gifts to either. The pain was just too much.

After living in Jacksonville for several years the company I worked for offered me a promotion which would take us back to Boston. The kids were 12 and 9 by then. I was excited for the job opportunity and thrilled to be going back home so I could be closer to my mom who was getting older.

Although many years had passed with little to no contact with my ex-husband, nor his family, once John and Melanie knew we would be moving back to Boston they decided they wanted to try and reconnect with their father. Unfortunately, in less than 6 weeks after we had moved back, he proved to be the same man he always was. Addiction was still prevalent in his life and he ended up hurting both of them so much they no longer wanted anything to do with him.

Now that the kids were older, there wasn't much I could do to shield them from the reality of who their biological father was. While they were younger and living in another state it offered a veil of protection. This was no longer an option.

They each dealt with the hurt and rejection in different ways. John pushed it to the side and focused on school and sports. Melanie's coping mechanisms went in an opposite and often unhealthier direction. While Melanie had a couple of great girlfriends, who remained best friends with her until her death, she also gravitated toward others who were going down a different path.

One day when she was barely a teenager, I received a call from the school letting me know she didn't show up for school that day. I was frantic and thought something bad had happened to her. I left work and began driving all over town looking for her and making phone calls to everyone we knew trying to find her. The hours ticked by and no one I knew had seen her. As it became later, and the day turned into night I was beside myself. A friend I touched base with earlier called me back and told me about a group of kids from a neighboring town. Apparently one of them had befriended Melanie and she thought Melanie might be there. This was long before GPS, Maps and Waze but somehow, I found my way to where this new friend lived. As I pulled up, there she was, standing in the middle of a large group of kids. This was only the beginning of Melanie searching for love and acceptance in all the wrong places.

She first sought that out in the person of her father, never understanding why he didn't want her nor love her. Throughout the years she would periodically touch base with him, only to be rejected again. During those teenage years as she became interested in boys, she wanted to have her person – someone who would love and accept her for herself. This would remain at the core of Melanie's issues her entire life.

John and Melanie were always the center of my world and I fondly referred to us as The Three Musketeers. I always felt it was the three of us against the world. As a single mom I worked hard to make ends meet. Because there was no child support or any other income to help us, I worked 50 – 60 hours a week, so there were many hours they were with my mom, a sitter or eventually when old enough, home alone.

One day I came home from work and John and Melanie couldn't wait for me to get out of the car as they greeted me at the back door. As they ushered me into the kitchen, I had been instructed to close my eyes as they had made me a present. When I opened my eyes, there on the table was a beautiful macaroni necklace. You know the kind – elbow macaroni which had been strung through a piece of rope with a bow tie on the ends. Oh, but *this* macaroni necklace was special! It had been painted with my brand-new bottle of OPI nail polish, which was now laying empty on its side on a white paper plate, with all the bristles of the brush facing every different direction. I'm so happy to say I still have that beautiful, special necklace today!

Moment of Reflection: Can you imagine how much our Heavenly Father loves his children? He sacrificed so much that He gave his only son for us.

CHAPTER 6

Man of the House

We went through many highs and lows during the teenage years. As any parent knows, this is an awkward stage in any child's life. It's one of self-awareness, development, discovery, and growth. It can be challenging even under the best of circumstances, but I believe more so for those who are single parents.

From the time John was a young boy he felt he had to take on the role as the man of the house. One night as I was heading out on a date, he told me he wanted me to take a test - it was called the napkin test. As I was thinking I'd never heard of such a thing, he proceeded to throw a napkin on the floor in front of me and instructed me to pick it up. When I did, he said, "Mom you need to go upstairs and change your shirt right away. When you bend down you can see things you're not supposed to." Ha-ha, so that's the old napkin test! Needless to say, I ran upstairs and changed!

John was the epitome of a big brother to Melanie. He tried his best to watch over her and be her protector, although she didn't always make it easy on him. He has a great sense of humor and would always be able to lighten things up and keep us laughing. He still has this gift today!

It wasn't until after Melanie ran ahead to heaven that John told me a story of the blanket game they played when they were very young. When it was time to clean up they would each grab hold of one end of the blanket and would continue folding it, getting closer and closer until at the very end when they were standing in front of one another, they would throw their arms around each other giggling like crazy, as they hugged.

One Mother's Day they decided to serve me breakfast in bed. They slowly came upstairs precariously balancing a tray, which held one silk red rose, and a plate filled with watery scrambled eggs, burnt toast and a cup of coffee that had splashed all over. After looking at those proud smiles I ate some of that breakfast no matter how it looked or tasted!

John and Melanie couldn't be more different than day is from night. Isn't that how it is in many families? Sure, there are some similarities, but this happens so often. Same set of parents – very different kids! This was true in our house as well.

One thing the two of them had in common was that God had given each of them incredibly generous, caring hearts and spirits. From a young age they each had a deep caring for other people and always wanted to help others. Certainly, there was a love of people, but they especially rooted for the underdog, wanted to help those less fortunate, and had a passion for ensuring fairness and respect for all. I so admired these qualities in them.

Even though aspects of our life were not easy for the three of us, the love was always there, no matter what the difficulty or circumstance. For that I am forever grateful. Melanie looked up to John her entire life and loved him so very much, right up until the day she died. Although addiction affects the entire family, and we were no different, underneath it all, love remains.

Somehow, we made it through the teenage years. It seems we were always in a constant struggle trying to keep Melanie interested in school. She wanted to quit school and get her GED instead.

There was no talking her out of this, and I had grown weary of fighting the daily battle of forcing her to attend each day, when she would just turn around and leave once she arrived. Eventually she got a job, bought her own car, and seemed to be on a good path. Melanie was dating a nice guy and seemed to finally be in a healthy relationship, with someone who genuinely cared about her. John graduated from college and we were all in a good place.

In 2002 I was blessed to receive another promotion. It was a great opportunity for my career, but the downside was I would have to leave Boston and move to Atlanta. I had never lived without my children before and even though they were 18 and 21 I still had a long moment of pause before accepting the position. I took some time to pray about it but knew in my heart this was the path God had for me. I would be leaving John and Melanie in Boston, living on their own.

Life was going along well for the first several months. I was flying home to Boston once a month to see the kids and my mom. Everything appeared to be going smoothly, although I would later reflect on this and wonder how I missed a few of the signs. Melanie was still in the same relationship but what I wasn't aware of was that her boyfriend began taking steroids. As his usage increased so did the bouts of rage he experienced. Suddenly, her healthy relationship began to take a deep dive and one day he pushed her down a flight of stairs. When she called to tell me, I went with my first instinct – get to a safe place and as far away from him as possible. So, I put her on a plane and brought her to Atlanta.

After a few weeks and many hours of conversation we realized it was time for a new start. She had always had a close relationship with two of her cousins who live in Jacksonville and we decided she would go live there for a while. She would have an opportunity to share an apartment with my niece, be around people her own age and have a new beginning. We were both so excited for this chance to start over. Unfortunately, if you aren't willing to deal with the core of a problem it doesn't matter how many times you change your zip code, these issues will follow you everywhere. It may take years, but it's all still there bubbling beneath the surface.

Moment of Reflection: Have you ever moved to another location only to find the same problem followed you there? Was it an eye opener and what did you do to resolve the problem?

CHAPTER 7

Appearances Can Be Deceiving

T he move to Atlanta didn't just bring a nice promotion and career boost, it brought me the love of my life, my husband Fred. We may think we know the plans for our life and then, God steps in and shows you He is the one directing your steps. *The steps of good men are directed by the Lord. He delights in each step they take (Psalm 37:23 TLB).* After having been a single mom for 20 years, we were married a year and half later and began enjoying our new life together.

Fred and I had both previously married at a very young age, so for the first time in our lives, our children were grown and we were enjoying life as empty nesters. Traveling is one of our great passions and we've been fortunate to visit many beautiful cities and countries around the world. We would wake up some days and say, "Where should we go this weekend?" And off we'd go! Life was good. About 4 years into our married life together things took a turn for which we were both ill prepared.

Melanie was still living in Jacksonville and seemed to be doing well. Things had been moving in a positive direction for a few years and we were grateful.

While Fred and I were vacationing in Maine with friends, we received an early morning call that Melanie had been in a car accident the night before. She was at the hospital and although seriously banged up had not suffered any life-threatening injuries. Unfortunately, Melanie had been charged with a DUI and was in serious legal trouble. I immediately flew from Maine to Jacksonville to assess the situation in person.

While partying with some friends Melanie discovered her boyfriend was cheating on her. Instead of remaining where she was or asking for a ride, she got in the car in an emotional state, along with having had some drinks, and lost control of her brand-new car as it went spinning headfirst into a palm tree in the median strip. Upon impact, the front of the car spun around and was crushed from the side. The car took on the shape of the letter "V" and had someone been with her in the passenger seat they would have died instantly. The driver's seat had been pushed backward and was found in the rear of the vehicle, with all the windows blown out. The only thing that remained untouched in the vehicle and in one piece was the driver's seat! Miraculously, Melanie was able to climb out of the vehicle through the rear window on her own but suffered back and neck injuries. Upon seeing the vehicle, I knew beyond a shadow of a doubt that God had indeed interceded and saved her that night.

Oh, we've all heard the saying, "a cat has nine lives." Well, Melanie was like the proverbial cat. I had often told her I never knew anyone who had gone through as many things as she had and survived. As the years went by, I would have a front row seat to how our Heavenly Father would spare her life many more times.

From the time my kids were little I would always pray this particular scripture verse over them, a portion of it comes from Psalm 91:11 and Isaiah 54:17 *"Lord, I command your angels to have charge over John and Melanie. No matter where they are or what they are doing, no weapon formed against them shall prosper, in Jesus' mighty name."* God's words are our weapons. We can and should use them to protect ourselves and our loved ones. There is no doubt God and his angels intervened in Melanie's life that night, and even though I didn't know what the future would hold, it wouldn't be the first time he came between her and death.

Some people have a life scripture – a scripture that has special meaning for them and is a guide for how they want to live their life. Melanie's life scripture was Jer. 29:11, *"For I know the plans I have for you," declares the* LORD, *"plans to prosper you and not to harm you, plans to give you hope and a future."* Melanie's heart's desire was to have hope and a wonderful future. Although she still had a personal relationship with Jesus, she wasn't walking with him in the way she knew she should. Thankfully, even when we may go our own way and momentarily turn our back on the Lord, he never turns his back on us.

Soon after the car accident Melanie was prescribed pain medication to combat the pain from the back injury she sustained. Although I didn't know it at the time, this was the beginning of the end as she soon became addicted to the pain medication the doctors continued to prescribe.

A couple of months passed by when Melanie got a new job, which she loved. She became friends with one of the facilitators who taught classes there and the friendship evolved into a relationship. On the outside everything appeared to be going along well and she seemed to once again be in a good place. Little did we know that she had begun consuming high amounts of pain pills and began to suffer from bleeding ulcers, along with having severe anxiety.

Her boyfriend was about 10 years older than she was and although level-headed and established in his career, he was also what Melanie described as "controlling." I was never certain about this because in Melanie's eyes anyone who attempted to guide her along the right path, including me, would appear to be controlling and she would rebel. As time went on, although he tried to help her, after a year and half of her impetuous behavior he suggested she move back home with us.

Moment of Reflection: Has there ever been a time in your life when you were certain God intervened in your life and saved you or a loved one? What did he do? Did it strengthen your relationship with him? Was it a source of encouragement for others to see his hand move so mightily?

CHAPTER 8

Rejection Roars

From Melanie's perspective the dissolution of this relationship was just another rejection. She was unaware I had received a call from her boyfriend to update me on what he had been witnessing. He believed she had developed an addiction to the prescription pain pills she was taking and although he loved her, it was much more than he could handle, and he felt she needed to be with family.

I knew he was right, but I also know my girl and she was going to view this as another abandonment. In her eyes it was another rejection, just like her biological father.

Although it was a tough conversation and many tears were shed, she agreed to come to Atlanta. So, after 5 years of living on her own Melanie came to live with us in April 2007. It also didn't take long before we were able to confirm she had indeed developed a serious addiction to the prescription medication she was taking.

She had been living with us for about a month when we got her a job at a friend's restaurant. This was one of the few restaurants that administered drug tests to their employees and provided a drug-free workplace. The hospitality industry is known for having a high degree of drug use and sadly, many restaurants do not even drug test their employees. Since the pills Melanie was taking were prescribed by a physician there was not a problem with passing the drug test. She was happy to get back to work, make a little money and stay busy.

As time went on, because Melanie was an adult and taking what was prescribed by a doctor, there wasn't much we could do to stop this. It was a battle we fought from the beginning as we tried to bring awareness that we believed the usage had drifted into abuse and had become a problem. We were left trying to figure out how to help her see this and wean off these pills that she believed she still needed.

We helped her enroll in the local community college and began talking more about the future. Melanie was the epitome of a caretaker and the medical field had always interested her. She wanted to be a nurse so we did all we could to get her started on this journey. We were very supportive, and during the first couple of months I thought we were making positive strides. Sadly, it didn't take long for things to begin to spiral downward. My friend called to let me know she was going to have to let Melanie go from the restaurant. There had been some erratic behavior and she believed she was using drugs. Unfortunately, Melanie connected with one of the few people who worked there who also had an appetite for pain pills. Not too long after this I could see that the new friends she made were not the best influence and things began to escalate at home.

We got into a very heated argument as I drove home from work one Friday night. She wanted to go to a party with this new group of friends, and instead of speaking rationally about it I gave her an ultimatum - dump the new friends and partying or find another place to live. Ever since Melanie was a child she was "Queen of the Strong-Willed Children." Let's just say my ultimatum didn't go over well. I'm sure I could have handled things better, but my patience and tolerance of the situation was deteriorating.

When I finally got home, my husband and I were getting ready to head out for an early dinner with friends. I was still fuming from my argument with Melanie, when she stormed in the back door, threw a purse she had borrowed toward me and ran upstairs. It happened so quickly that I didn't even see her face or have a chance to respond.

For the first time ever, when we left the house, I didn't say goodbye but simply walked out. This may not sound like anything unusual to you, but this was not something we did in our home. We never went to bed angry and whenever we were leaving the house, we always said goodbye and I love you. Not this time.

Over the years I have learned to recognize the promptings of the Holy Spirit. Some people call it their gut, instinct, or the gift of discernment. As a Christian, when Jesus was living on this earth, he told the disciples he would be going soon but he would leave them with a Comforter (John 14:16). This is the Holy Spirit. For as long as I can remember, discernment is one of the gifts God has given me and this particular Friday night of July 15, 2007 was no different.

As we sat and ate dinner, I knew in my gut something was wrong. I couldn't wait for dinner to be over and go home. I was still upset about my argument with Melanie and worried that she was going to that party with this new group of friends, who were nothing but trouble in my eyes.

When we got home Melanie's car was in the driveway, so I assumed she got a ride. As we opened the back door from the garage, the house was in total darkness and the door leading up to Melanie's room was swung wide open, instead of being closed as it normally was. I began calling her name but received no answer. Since the house was in total darkness I figured she was gone, but something compelled me to go upstairs. As I reached the top of the stairs and turned the light on , I saw her body laying across the bed sideways. She didn't answer when I called her name, and when I climbed on the bed and touched her, she began mumbling incoherently. I immediately knew she had taken something and said, "Oh, Melanie what did you take?" I was trying to talk to her and wake her up, but she only continued to mumble. I was able to turn her body around the right way in the bed, laying her head on the pillow. As I began to pull the covers over her, it was at that moment when I saw them - multiple pill bottles scattered all over the floor of the room, along with 2 pieces of paper. When I picked the paper up and read the first two lines, I realized it was a suicide note.

I fled down the stairs as quickly as my legs would take me, running to get my phone out of my purse, all the while yelling for my husband.

I called 911 and although they kept me on the phone until they arrived, I immediately began praying over Melanie as she lay there, claiming she would live and not die.

Moment of Reflection: Have you ever had something rise up on the inside of you, one of those gut instinct moments? We are often so busy going through life it's easy to miss those Holy Spirit moments. Has it made you more aware to pay attention to that still small voice inside of you?

CHAPTER 9

The Brink of Death

I t wasn't until I was sitting in the Emergency Room that I realized how serious the situation with Melanie had become. I didn't see how deep the hurt was about her broken relationship, and I didn't realize how strong her addiction had become to the prescription pain pills. Was I naïve? I didn't think so. Was I in denial? Possibly. Or was I just a mother who loved her only daughter, and even in the middle of the storm continued to see the good and believe the best? Whatever the reason, I was about to have the rose-colored glasses I may have been wearing ripped from my eyes.

Since there were multiple bottles strewn around her bedroom, we didn't know exactly how many pills Melanie had consumed. In addition, there seemed to be several different types of prescriptions also. As we waited to get an update a nurse came out and escorted us to a private room. I didn't know it at the time, but Melanie was in the room next to us as they continued working to save her life.

At some point during the wait I knew we needed reinforcements, so I left the room to call a few friends who were prayer warriors. At the exact moment I stepped into the hallway someone flung open the door to the room next to us and that was when I saw my daughter's naked body lying on a table, head thrown back, tubes seeming to come from everywhere, as medical personnel filled the tiny room while continuing to feverishly work on her. It's a picture in my mind I will never forget.

More than 3 hours after we arrived a doctor finally came and joined us in our room. He told us Melanie was on life support and would be taken to ICU. He explained that things didn't look promising due to the vast number of drugs she had in her system and we should be prepared to say goodbye to her. I had to ask him to repeat what he said because I couldn't believe what I was hearing. He was very compassionate as he once again explained the situation to us. As we left that tiny room we were numb and in shock as we walked like zombies alongside her bed making our way to ICU.

Once they got her settled, they allowed us to come back into the room. Her nurse was a kind and sweet person, but it was obvious she had been told to prepare me for the inevitable. "I'm so very sorry. I know it must be very hard for you to see your daughter this way. I've been a nurse for a long time and I've never seen anyone who took both the amount and type of drugs that Melanie has in her system come out of it. As difficult as it is, you should begin to prepare yourself in case she doesn't recover."

I was sitting on the top of a small, square brown table, as I leaned against the wall when she said these words. I remember looking at her like she was a unicorn. Simply unbelievable! Other than the swooshing sound of the machine that was breathing for my girl, it was quiet in those first few moments after she stopped talking. This was all so surreal, but there was something I had absolutely no trouble remembering and that is who I was – a believer in Jesus Christ! A mother who believed in the power of God! And just as I had prayed over Melanie in her bedroom while waiting for the EMT's, I let that nurse know exactly who she was dealing with and that I believed Melanie was going to live and not die. I told her from that moment on there would be no negative talk in Melanie's room.

My husband and I left the hospital to come home for an hour to get some things. I laid down on our bed just to close my eyes for a moment, when all of a sudden I began hearing a few words from the song "Praise You In This Storm" by Mercy Me: *"Every tear I've cried you hold in your hand, You never left my side and though my heart is torn, I will praise you in this storm."* I hadn't heard the song recently and didn't understand why it was playing like a record in my mind now, but something made me sit up and scribble the words down on a piece of paper, which I then threw in the nightstand drawer.

On a side note, this would be the first of many times when I would begin to wake in the middle of the night and get different song lyrics in my spirit. I began keeping a pen and paper beside my bed and would scribble down some of the words so I would remember them when I woke up in the morning. This has continued throughout the years, and although I thought it was odd, every time it happened I would get up and plug the words into my phone to see what the name of the song was. (Thank you, Google!) They were always words of encouragement that would minister to my soul. Imagine my surprise when I came across a scripture one day in Job 35:10 that says, *"Where is God my maker, who gives me songs in the night."* God loves his children so much. He can deliver messages of love and encouragement through music and song as a means to provide hope and healing.

We didn't stay home long, but when we went back to the hospital I was armed. I had my Bible, a portable CD player, Christian music CD's, Melanie's favorite lotion and the Chapstick she would go nowhere without. The neurologist came in early that morning to see her. He was a very kind doctor who had a good reputation and had been practicing for many years. After examining Melanie, he asked us to step outside. "I want you to know we have done everything we can medically do for Melanie. It is out of our hands now and is up to God." He continued, "With the type of drugs Melanie ingested she could wake up a vegetable, if she wakes up at all." Although those are very sobering words to hear I refused to receive any of it. I recall responding, "Thank you, but I do not believe that. We are standing on the word and promises of God and will believe for a miracle." He smiled and went on his way. From that point forward, I continually played Christian music as I walked around the room, praying over my girl. Melanie was also being lifted up in prayer by many people all over the country. Was I a fanatic about it? Yes, I was, but when you need a miracle you become a fanatic! I was a determined, passionate mom looking to Jesus to heal my daughter.

Late into the second day, an old friend from Jacksonville was returning from a prayer conference and coming through Atlanta. She had heard about Melanie and asked if she could stop by the hospital and pray with us. When she arrived, Fred, John and I were the only ones in the room. We all gathered around Melanie's bed, laying hands on her as we prayed. I wish I could remember exactly what prayers we prayed over her that afternoon, but what I do remember is that the Holy Spirit was present in that room. After my friend finished praying, she left to continue her drive home.

One of the main things the doctors were troubled by was that Melanie's blood pressure continued to be dangerously low. When she arrived at the hospital it was 50/30. They had been giving her multiple medications to try and stabilize her blood pressure but every time they tried to make any adjustments it would plummet. A couple of hours after our friend left, we were standing in Melanie's room when suddenly, her nurse told me to look up at the monitor.

When I did her blood pressure read, 125/70 and she said, "Gee, you think someone was praying in here!" A miracle had indeed taken place and God had begun healing Melanie! She soon began to wake up and was removed from the ventilator. She was their miracle girl. Several of the nurses came by to see her and couldn't believe it, but I sure could! The doctor wasn't certain if her mind and memory would be affected by the drugs down the road, but when God does something, he does it all the way and he does it with excellence.

My girl not only woke up, but she was not cognitively impaired, nor a vegetable as the doctor said she could be. She was healed and whole. Oh, how thankful I was for his miracle saving power! This was now the second time God had saved Melanie from the brink of death, but it would not be the last.

Moment of Reflection: God is our waymaker, miracle worker, and promise keeper. Have you had a time in your life where there was no denying he alone made something come to pass? Is music an inspiration to you in your life? Does God give you songs in the night?

CHAPTER 10

A New Beginning

After Melanie's suicide attempt, we began getting her the help she so desperately needed. I'm not going to say it was easy because it wasn't, but I began to feel hopeful. She continued taking classes at the local community college, got a job and began working a program. We were connected as a family, began doing mother-daughter things together and love and laughter again began to permeate our world. We entered a season of normalcy and although I would watch her closely to ensure the darkness remained at bay, life was looking brighter than it had in a long while.

Melanie had a deep love for her stepdad, and I will always be forever grateful that Fred has always loved both of my children as if they were his own flesh and blood. After Melanie died I came across this note she sent to him on Father's Day 2019. What a beautiful gift and treasure it is:

Hey Dad,

Happy Father's Day. I know I haven't been around the past few years to wish you a Happy Father's Day, but I just wanted you to know how much I love you and appreciate you. You have been a part of my life for so long now and have ALWAYS been who I look to as my father. Thank you for trying to guide me in the right direction and loving me no matter what decision I've made. Thank you for loving Cameron as much as you do and teaching him how to be the good man that I know he will become! Last but not least... My Mother... Thank you for loving her the way you do. Happy Father's Day! I love you!

In Fred's eyes there is no difference between those who share his blood line and those of his kids who don't. He is an exceptional husband, father, and human being. God knew what our Three Musketeers, plus one would need, and he brought them the best of the best in the form of a godly man to be their Dad. The love Melanie so desperately wanted from her biological father and never received may have been at the center of her hurt, but she was finally experiencing what it was like to have a real Dad and was able to see firsthand how a man should treat a woman. How bittersweet it was when I came across a handwritten note from her after she ran ahead to heaven, that said, *"Dad, I will love you forever. Your daughter, Melanie"* Yes, he had made a positive, loving impact on a girl who had yet to feel that kind of unconditional love from a man.

Several months after Melanie's suicide attempt, she continued on a positive path, and while attending an NA meeting she met Tommy. He was also in recovery and although we tried to encourage her to focus on her future, and not engage in pursuing a relationship with someone who also struggled with the disease of addiction, there was no stopping this train from leaving the station.

So, instead of letting this become an issue between us, we embraced them both and encouraged each of them on their journey. What we saw were two kids who had made some mistakes along the way but were trying hard to do the right thing. We became like second parents to Tommy, whose parents lived in another state. We tried to provide a good, healthy example of life and what it means to be in a loving relationship. Overall, things were going well, and we were once again, hopeful.

A couple of years into the relationship Melanie discovered she was pregnant. I remember so clearly the day she found out. By this time, I had recently taken early retirement and was enjoying a freedom I'd never experienced before.

It was a beautiful September day, and I was standing in the kitchen when she came around the corner with an odd look on her face. I immediately knew something was up and stopped what I was doing. When I asked her what was wrong she said, "Momma, I'm pregnant." She told me she was scared and wasn't sure she'd be a good mother. I quickly wrapped my arms around her, and quietly said, "Melanie, you have so much love to give. You'll make a great mom! You are not alone, and we will do this together." Maybe the timing wasn't perfect, but I encouraged her every step of the way. I was also very excited at the prospect of becoming a grandmother!

Tommy proposed and they planned on getting married sometime after the baby was born. Little did I know when I took early retirement the plans God would have for us all. This would be one of the best things I would be doing with my newfound freedom. I was thrilled to be able to share this joy with Melanie and made myself available to be there for her. When Tommy couldn't go, I attended every doctor appointment with her, and we excitedly began planning for the baby's arrival. We soon found out she was going to have a boy and wanted to name him Cameron. Every month we would take a photo of her belly to see how much she had grown and how big Cameron was getting. We indulged every craving and tried to encourage her all along the way. This was one of the happiest times of her life and I loved sharing each special moment with my girl.

Since Melanie's closest friends lived in Boston, I planned two baby showers for her – one back in Boston, and another here in Atlanta. We had such fun celebrating with our family and friends in both places.

During the latter part of the pregnancy we began to see some cracks in the relationship with Tommy but attributed it to the stresses and strains of life. Melanie wasn't working and Tommy had a minimum wage job, so we knew money was a constant pressure. A couple of months before the baby was due to arrive we helped them find an apartment close to where we lived and helped fill it with all the things they would need to have a good start together as a family of 3.

Finally, in May 2009, our sweet Cameron was born. Melanie asked me to be with her during the birth. What an honor, privilege and lifetime blessing it is to see your child give birth to her child!

Melanie, Tommy, and Cameron all came back to stay at our house for the first 2 weeks so she could recover and get some help with the baby, since Tommy wouldn't be able to take any time off work. We were more than happy to have them all stay with us and were overjoyed to have our sweet Cameron in the house. Whatever was going on before Cameron was born seemed to straighten itself out and they were happy. I once again had such high hopes.

Then barely two months after Cameron was born, Melanie came and asked if they could move in with us as they could no longer afford their apartment. Melanie was not working, and Tommy's salary couldn't cover their housing expenses.

Moment of Reflection: New beginnings and hope go hand in hand. How thankful we are for second chances. When have you experienced a time where God gave you a second chance? Was there a time when the impossible turned possible? Sometimes it's hard to see and that's when I remember the scripture from *Isaiah 43:19, "I am doing something brand new, something unheard of. Even now it sprouts and grows and matures. Don't you perceive it? I will make a way in the wilderness and open up flowing streams in the desert."*

CHAPTER 11

The Unraveling

I wish I could say the move to our house made things better but unfortunately, it began a downward spiral for both Melanie and Tommy.

About 3 months after Cameron was born I went back to work full time. The moment I would get home from work Cameron became my responsibility since Melanie said she needed a break after taking care of the baby all day. When Tommy got home from work he was too tired to "babysit." As we approached Cameron's first birthday we began to see a familiar pattern developing and noticed behavior changes in both of them that frightened me. It didn't take long for us to realize they both had begun self-medicating, which made us very concerned about leaving Cameron alone with them. Soon Cameron began sleeping in our room on a nightly basis. They obviously enjoyed the freedom and sleep, and we allowed it to continue because we no longer trusted them to take good care of him.

We encouraged them to begin going back to NA and they agreed this would be a good idea. Each evening after dinner they would leave to attend a meeting and instead would return high.

As more time passed we began missing items from the house – tools, coins, electronics, money and even credit cards. It was a way of life we knew nothing about, but we were getting a good education, for sure. We soon found out they were stealing our things and pawning them to get money to pay for drugs. It got to the point where we installed locks on our bedroom door and would lock up anything of value. It literally became a living hell in our own home!

We found evidence of the prescription drugs they were using, along with discovering hundreds of scratch tickets in an old shoebox in the back of the closet. It amounted to hundreds of dollars they could have used to support themselves, instead they were living with us while we supported everyone and took care of Cameron, too.

Unfortunately, this behavior is the desperate act of those who have the disease of addiction. This is not an excuse – this is reality. I didn't understand it at the time as Melanie had never done these things before, but I have a better understanding of it all now.

When Cameron was 15 months old Melanie and Tommy's relationship had deteriorated to the point where they were breaking up and Tommy decided to move to Florida to start anew. Melanie was so angry she told me "Mom, I didn't have a baby with you and Dad. Why does he get to leave, and I'm stuck here?"

After Tommy left Melanie wanted to take a weekend trip to Boston to see a girlfriend. I thought a little getaway might be just what she needed. Hopefully after spending time with her two best friends maybe they would be able to talk some sense into her, and she would come home renewed and refreshed, missing her baby. Instead, after she came home, her behavior was stranger than before she left. Apparently, when she went to Boston she didn't spend much time with her two best friends but connected with some old friends who were not the best influence.

Within 2 months after Tommy left for Florida, Melanie announced she was moving back to Boston under the pretense of "getting her life together." The most shocking part of it all was that she wasn't taking Cameron with her, but rather asked if I would take temporary guardianship of him while she was gone. She finally admitted she relapsed and had begun taking prescription pain pills again. She said giving her this time away alone was what she needed. "I can't do it here, Mom. My friend is a great support, and she will help me get back on my feet. I have to do this so I can be a good mother to Cameron."

During the weeks before she was scheduled to leave, our daily conversation consisted of me trying to convince her to stay. This was one of the saddest times of my life and I was completely devastated. Considering I had been a single mom for over 20 years, no matter how difficult things were, I never once considered leaving my children. But there was no talking her out of it. In her mind she truly believed that giving me temporary guardianship of Cameron and moving back to Boston was the right thing for her. I wondered, did she really believe she could get clean and sober up there and come back home?

Two days before she was due to leave we stood in the kitchen like cowboys in a standoff. She was on one side and I was on the other, both of our arms crossed in front of us. I begged and pleaded with her not to do this. Leaving her child would be the biggest mistake of her entire life and doing so would permanently alter both her life and Cameron's.

She knew Cameron would be safe with me and in her mind, it was like leaving him with a babysitter. She wasn't *really* leaving him – she was just taking a trip for a while, to get better. Well, that's the lie she told herself. From my perspective, she was listening to all the wrong people and she was indeed making the worst mistake of her life.

It was at this juncture that her brother, John, intervened and tried his best to talk some sense into her. He also begged her not to do this. He wrote her a long letter and sent me a copy. As I read how he pleaded for her to reconsider, offering his help and support toward recovery, my heart shattered for us all. In John's eyes, she was doing exactly what their biological father had done to them – he left and walked out. He knew she would regret it, but his words also fell on deaf ears. This moment in time and the decision Melanie made would change the course of their entire relationship for years to come. Whether it was right or wrong, after Melanie left Cameron, John did not speak to her except for a handful of times over 8 long years.

He saw the immense hurt her decision had caused our family and could not forgive her for it. Thankfully after many years they were able to find a way toward healing the year before Melanie died. For this I am eternally grateful.

The morning Melanie left, as I drove her to the airport it was as if I was engulfed in a thick, heavy fog. I remained in disbelief and felt like a zombie. Even during the short 30-minute drive to the airport, I once again begged her not to go. "Melanie, we can turn this car around and go home right now. We can get you the help you need here. You don't have to go to Boston to get help." It was as if I was speaking to the air or better yet, a brick wall. She hopped out of the car like she was leaving on vacation, and at that moment my life changed in a way I had never envisioned.

Subsequently, at the age when most of our friends were grand-parents and empty nesters, my husband and I became parents again. We were shell-shocked to say the least and it was a turning point in our lives. Astonishingly, there are an estimated 2.7 million grandparents raising their grandchildren today in the United States alone.

Moment of Reflection: Has your life ever taken a drastic turn which you had never anticipated? Was it as a result of someone else's choices but you suffered the consequence? How did you handle it? What steps did you take to regain control of your world?

CHAPTER 12

Freefall

I wish I could say this dream of Melanie's became a reality and she did get her life together and returned home clean and sober. But that wasn't the case.

Melanie continued living in Boston while Fred and I were becoming reaccustomed to being full time parents again. There is a reason God designed us to have babies when we are young.

Even though we had both retired, we had gone on to have second careers and were working. I had never intended on going back to work full time, but instead figured I'd get a part-time job in our local community. As I look at things in hindsight, God knew what was going to happen in our lives and was preparing the way even though I didn't realize it then.

A job opportunity working for one of the top 3 companies I had on my short list came my way. Even though it wasn't part time it was a great opportunity to work for a company that had the same values I did, and in a culture that supported everything I believed in. They also had an onsite day care, which at this stage of our lives was a huge benefit for us. Cameron could drive to work with me in the morning, and I could even have lunch with him during the day if my schedule permitted. I knew he was being well taken care of and was also learning so many things during his time there. It was so much more than daycare, and the fact that it was also in a

Christian environment was amazing! We would drive home singing the new songs he learned, and he would tell me all about his adventures with his friends! Out of all of us, Cameron was the one who was doing the best. He was thriving in his new environment and that made all the difference during this difficult season.

Even though he was only 18 months old when Melanie left, during those first few weeks when she was gone there was a definite sadness about him. As I've looked at pictures from that time I notice a distinct sadness in his eyes in a few of the photos. I'm sure somewhere in his sweet, young mind he was wondering where his Mommy went.

Fred and I were determined to live our best lives, in our new normal. Melanie had been gone more than a month when Thanksgiving was upon us. We decided we were going to visit friends in Naples, Florida. Cameron had never been on a plane before and I was able to capture the most adorable picture of him standing on his tiptoes peering out the window, as he was barely tall enough to see outside. Our friends were so gracious welcoming us into their home. Even though we continued to press on, I know emotionally, we were a shell of ourselves.

Even during this time God continued to shine his light onto our path and gave us treasured memories we will take with us forever. The most precious one being that Cameron finally said my name!

I know all parents think their kids are the smartest, prettiest, most handsome children ever born and we were no different! Cameron was a very smart little boy and began walking and talking at a very early age, but the one thing he had not yet said was my name. He spoke in short phrases and sentences, yet he would not say the one word I longed to hear - Grammy! I would get in front of his face and say, "Ga-Ga-Ga-Grammy. Say it, Cameron. Grammy!"

Oh, he would laugh and smile, then run away! On Thanksgiving Day, while at our friend's home I was standing in the living room when from out of nowhere I heard this little voice yell, "Honneeyy!!" When I turned around our sweet little boy was standing in the kitchen, hands on his hips, looking at me with the biggest smile on his face. It took only a fraction of a second to realize he was calling me – Honey! We have assumed he heard Fred call me that, but I believe it was a Godwink. Although I didn't know it then, I was not going to be a Grammy to this beautiful boy, so he blessed me with a very special name to seal our special relationship. It was one of the sweetest moments in my life, and from that day forward, I've been Honey ever since.

While there was still a heaviness over that first holiday without Melanie, there was also beauty among the broken pieces. Cameron had his first plane ride, his first beach visit (he didn't like the sand on his feet), and his first time in a pool. He loved running through the splash pad as the water poured over his beautiful red hair. Yes, even during a storm, God can provide glimpses of beauty and joy.

As Christmas approached Melanie asked if she could come home to see Cameron for the holiday. Although I was still dealing with so many thoughts and feelings which I hadn't even begun to process, I didn't deny her request. It was a very uncomfortable time as we all tried to ignore the emotions that were bubbling underneath the surface. It felt like Mt. Vesuvius waiting to erupt.

I thought Cameron would be excited to see his Mommy but instead he ran and clung to me. She was devastated, although I wasn't sure what she was expecting from him after being gone for a couple of months. During this time, it took all I had within me to walk in love as I knew Jesus would want me to do.

Shortly before she was due to return to Boston she received a call from the friend she was living with. The next thing I knew she was crying and said she was no longer welcome to live there. All this drama was a typical way of life for Melanie. I don't know how she managed to endure this lifestyle for as long as she did because the turmoil and uncertainty alone made me crazy. In the end, they resolved whatever the issue was and soon after Christmas ended she went back to Boston.

Since Melanie now lived out of state I often had to take her word for how things were going. I was still holding out hope that she would wake up and return to Atlanta, and to Cameron. I continued covering her in prayer as I knew deep down inside of me things were not going as well as she would have liked me to believe. The one thing I was certain of, she was not getting clean and sober in Boston.

Except for me, Melanie stopped talking with all those who knew her best and loved her most. She developed an entirely new group of friends and although she was now living in the same city as her two best friends, she rarely reached out to them. She would call to speak with Cameron, but those calls were brief and very one-sided.

Though I didn't approve of Melanie's choices, there was still the heart of a mother who was deeply concerned for her daughter as it became more and more obvious things were getting worse, and not better. Unfortunately, I soon found out that Melanie was sinking deeper into her addiction, going from prescription pain pills to heroin.

Moment of Reflection: Have you had the opportunity to look at something in hindsight and realize it was God's hand that was making a better path for you? Do you think this influenced how you may deal with other challenges you faced at another time?

CHAPTER 13

God's Girl

O ne day I received a call from Melanie. She was in a very dark place and at the end of her rope. She confided in me how bad things were. Her relationship had ended, she was deeply depressed, and wanted to end her life. She also couldn't believe she had left her baby and not only wasn't clean and sober but was now addicted to heroin.

My heart was broken for her, but all my love wasn't going to solve this problem. Melanie needed professional help, and she needed to find her way back to the Lord. She had given her life to him when she was younger but after leaving Cameron she outwardly rejected anything having to do with God. She blamed him for the demise of her relationships and the reason why things never seemed to work out in her life.

After several long talks, Melanie agreed to go into a detox facility in Boston, followed by rehab. Once she was released from detox she would return to Atlanta and go directly into a long-term program. These were all good decisions, but the biggest hurdle was finding a place.

Thankfully, there was a detox facility available close to where Melanie was staying that had an open bed. Since I was over 1000 miles away I arranged for a friend to pick her up and drop her off.

When Melanie completed detox, my dear friend picked her back up and put her on a plane to Atlanta.

One of the greatest struggles we have in our society today is the lack of good rehabs. And if you don't have medical insurance that creates an even greater layer of complexity. I know parents who have spent hundreds of thousands of dollars on rehabs. We spent plenty of money trying to help Melanie, but we were not willing to bankrupt ourselves to send her to an expensive rehab, especially now that we had a young child we were responsible for raising. We need good, affordable care that offers medical intervention, in addition to psychological, and emotional support, as well as a spiritual component to help create a well-rounded means of care.

Finding adequate and affordable rehab facilities for our children is not like the shows we see on television. It takes a lot of time, research, and money to find reputable places that are going to pour into our loved ones and provide the help that is needed. There is also not a magic 30-day program. From my experience it requires a minimum of 90 days and up to 1 year is recommended.

I figured I had about one week before Melanie would be released from detox and once she was I'd better have a place for her to go. In between working and taking care of Cameron this became my focus.

Melanie would call me once a day from the detox facility. She was always very emotional. I knew so little about heroin, but learned it effects both the physical and mental part of a person's body. I could only imagine what detoxing must feel like. On two occasions she had to leave me a voicemail. I don't remember saving them, but after she died I found these voice mails tucked away in a file on an old computer. Little did I know when I saved them 8 years before that listening to these voicemails today and hearing her voice would be a treasured gift. Once again, God have me a glimpse of beautiful in the middle of the broken.

After a multitude of hours researching and reaching out to many facilities I was able to find availability at a faith-based rehab in South Georgia. It was a one-year program and although she wasn't thrilled about this, I felt this would be a good place for her to get the help she needed.

The rehab was in an old Victorian home on a dirt road in the middle of nowhere. Once you made it to the end of the road it opened up to all these old, magnificent trees with Spanish moss hanging off each limb. There was a donkey running around in back and the house had a lovely front porch filled with rocking chairs and a big swing. As we pulled up in front, several women came running out to greet us and welcome Melanie. The director, Sandy, came bounding down the steps with the biggest smile and threw her arms around Melanie. She was wearing a t-shirt that said, "God's Girl." She was a former addict who had been sober for several years and was now giving back to other women who needed help. It seemed like a nice place, with a decent program and I just prayed Melanie would embrace it and get better.

One of the rules of the house was that I wouldn't be able to speak with Melanie for the first 30 days. As I drove away, looking in the rearview mirror it took everything within me to not turn around, scoop her back up and take her home with me. All I wanted was to love and protect my girl, but I knew she needed more than a momma's love could provide. I prayed I had made the right choice.

While no rehab is perfect – at least I never found one that was, Melanie managed to remain in this program for 7 months. She worked through a lot of issues and it was also during this time she gave her life back to the Lord and began a heartfelt relationship with

Him. Even years after leaving this place it was her time here that we would often talk about and reflect upon. She knew that keeping God at the center of her recovery was her best hope to remain on the right path.

Moment of Reflection: Were there times you wondered if you had made the right decision or second-guessed yourself? What did you do? How did you handle this?

CHAPTER 14

Another Curve in the Road

O nce Melanie left rehab she was ready to embark on what she called a "normal" life. Yet she hadn't lived a normal life for quite a few years. She had spent the better part of 2 years trapped in her addiction and then went into rehab, which was like a warm, protective cocoon. Patience was never Melanie's strongest suit but trying to slow down a moving train is near impossible. She wanted everything back to normal, now!

She got a used car so she could get a job and go back and forth to work. She was working in the hospitality industry again and started to make a little money of her own. She was attending church with us, attending NA meetings, and starting to meet a few people her own age. She even continued journaling as she had done while in rehab. This was a good, positive outlet for her to express her thoughts and feelings. Many months after Melanie died I found several of her journals among her things.

We continued to encourage rebuilding her relationship with Cameron, but it was hard for him to receive any kind of instruction or discipline from someone who was very much a stranger to him. Melanie had a hard time understanding this. The only thing she knew was she was his mommy and she expected him to recognize that. Unfortunately, being a mommy is more than a name or title. It's a relationship and a role, and Melanie had been gone so long he never remembered her in this role. In Cameron's eyes I was his mommy. I was the one who was there when he had a bad dream, or was sick, scared, tired, or happy. Fred and I were the constants in his life. As hard as we tried to explain this to Melanie she couldn't seem to understand it from our point of view.

Melanie reconnected with her cousin and one weekend they took a trip to visit my sister. She enjoyed this time away and being on my sister's farm. She was also proud to show off her jam-making skills. They made more jam and canned more veggies than she had ever done before! While she had a wonderful time, I later found out some of her conversation indicated she had a lot of resentment toward me, and unfortunately, that resentment would simmer just below the surface. Years later we would finally have the chance to talk about this, and she admitted it wasn't so much that she resented my relationship with Cameron but was angry with herself for leaving him. It was an unfortunate consequence of her decision to leave that resulted in how he related to her, which was not as a mother, but more like a sister. Although she came to understand this much later it was something that hurt her terribly.

After a period of time, I began to see a change in Melanie's behavior. Once again the magnet was pulling her back into her old life. Soon she stopped working her program and began falling back into old habits.

We lived like this for several months but eventually we had to ask Melanie to leave our home as she was no longer living a sober lifestyle and we didn't want Cameron living in this environment. She didn't really have anywhere to go and the tension in the house was so bad it got to the point where we rented an apartment just to get her out from underneath our roof. I couldn't believe it had come to this, but we felt as if we had no other choice. She was working so we had her sign a contract with us and she agreed to take over the lease within 6 months. I like to think we were hopeful that things would work out, but honestly, at that point the stress of her addiction made it clear that we could no longer live under the same roof any longer.

By the time the lease was up six months later she not only didn't hold up her end of the agreement, but she was also involved with a crowd that terrified me. During this time, she had many people staying in the apartment with her. It had become a hangout and place to go, for which we were footing the bill. Though we tried to get her to return to rehab she flat out refused. She had absolutely no interest in recovery during this time. It is impossible to save someone who doesn't want to be saved, and it's one of the most helpless feelings in the world.

Needless to say, we did not renew the lease. This was the beginning of a period when my beautiful girl, who I barely recognized anymore, became homeless and began couch surfing with her boyfriend. Eventually she would end up living on the street.

Moment of Reflection: What do you do when you feel backed up against a wall with no means of escape?

CHAPTER 15

Difficult Life –
Changing Decisions

E ven though Melanie was no longer living in the apartment
I continued to support her in many ways. It would take
me a few more years before I would get to a place where I was no
longer enabling her. This is a fine line for parents. Do we continue
supporting them financially for things that support a drug-free
life? What if she was hungry? What if she was cold? Do I buy her a
winter coat? There were so many, many nights I would lay in bed
with my eyes wide open looking around our bedroom. I was warm
and comfortable tucked into a king size bed with a warm blanket
covering me. Where was my girl sleeping? Was she sleeping on
the bathroom floor of a local gas station? Was she safe? Here I was
living in a nice home and she was living on the street. Night after
night I would lay there waiting for my phone to ring with the news
no parent wants to hear.

As Melanie began to sink deeper into her addiction, we knew
we needed to protect Cameron, so we hired an attorney and began
proceedings to legally adopt him. Melanie was not in Cameron's life
very much during this time since she was rarely in any condition
to be around him. Every time we talked I continued to offer her the
option of rehab, but she adamantly declined the offer.

There are many moments in a person's life that remain unforgettable. This was about to be another one of those moments for me. I asked Melanie if she would please come to the house, but she had to agree to come sober. Once she arrived we sat in the dining room as I explained what we wanted to do for Cameron – we wanted to officially adopt him. She began to pace around the table, then sat down and began crying. "Mom, this isn't what I want but I know in my heart this is the best thing for Cameron. I don't know how I got here but I know I can't take care of him. I know you and Dad love him and will give him the life I can't." It was one of the hardest things she did, but it was also the best thing she could have done for her boy.

In the State of Georgia, since Melanie was not married to Cameron's biological father we did not need his permission to adopt Cameron, but we did attempt to do the right thing and obtain his agreement. By then, Tommy had not seen Cameron in a couple of years and was also still active in his addiction. He never showed up for scheduled visits and would only call on holidays and birthdays. Tommy made little to no effort to have a relationship with Cameron for more than 2 years, so we were surprised at his reaction when we let him know we were officially adopting Cameron. Our main goal was to protect Cameron from both of his biological parents who were continuing to use drugs during this time and were unable to care for him.

When Cameron was 4 years old it became official! He proudly sat on the judge's knee and signed his own name on the adoption papers! It was a touching and yet bittersweet moment for us. We feel so blessed to have another son. And even though we weren't expecting to be parents again, being an older parent has many benefits. When I was younger and raising John and Melanie there were so many pressures, along with the added stress of being a single parent. This time around, I have a wonderful partner, and we are older and wiser. We can do so much with Cameron and have been able to travel all over the world with him. He's barely a teenager and he's already visited multiple countries and more than half of the United States. But more importantly he is loved and safe.

Moment of Reflection: When you've had to make a difficult decision what is your first instinct? Do you begin to pray about it, seeking the Lord's face? Do you have a trusted family member or friend who can help lead and guide you?

CHAPTER 16

Here Comes the Judge

Melanie's addiction continued to take her down many dark paths, and although she hated who she had become she could not seem to find her way forward. We always kept in close contact, either by text or phone daily.

We all find our own ways to parent and many parents of addicted children go the tough love route. I did not believe in this approach and never cut her off emotionally. It took time, but I eventually learned not to enable her, but instead always reinforced that I loved her unconditionally and would be here for her when she decided she wanted help. Although I didn't give her money, I did provide her with a cell phone to ensure as a woman living on the street she would have a way to call for help if she needed it. And when we talked I would always ask, "Melanie, are you ready yet? Have you had enough yet, honey?" I always told her when she was ready to get help I would come get her no matter where she was or what time, day, or night.

One day while I was in prayer for Melanie, God impressed upon my heart that I needed to treat her with compassion. Melanie didn't want to be this way. She didn't want to be addicted to drugs. Who would? This wasn't her dream life! It wasn't much of a life at all, chasing one high to another just to avoid being sick. But finding a way out isn't easy once you're so far down this long, dark road. As I prayed that day something changed in me, and from that moment on the Lord turned all the anger and resentment I'd been carrying around deep inside me for my daughter, into compassion and love.

With the disease of addiction comes a host of many other problems including legal issues. My daughter was no exception. She spent time in jail on several occasions. I was so ashamed by this it would be a long time before I would ever tell anyone, other than a very small handful of close friends who walked this journey with us.

One of the saddest things was, as much as I tried, Melanie knew I was ashamed of this part of her life. Addiction does not just affect the addict – it affects the entire family! Shame is one of the stigmas associated with this disease. Melanie was so ashamed of herself and there was a part of me that could relate. I loved her so much, but there was nothing I could do to change her. It is the most helpless feeling in the world. Many times, I didn't even want to discuss the details with my intimate group of friends who I trusted. It was that shameful and disheartening to me.

One day Melanie ended up being in the wrong place at the wrong time. When the police showed up they ran everyone's name through the system and discovered she had an outstanding warrant out against her due to a probation violation. When she appeared in court, she ended up going before a judge whom she had appeared before previously. The judge was aware that the root of Melanie's issue was her disease of addiction. It had been her hope he would allow her to be released into a day program where she could receive outpatient drug treatment. Instead, he told Melanie, "I was going to let you make the decision about whether you wanted to go to an intensive outpatient program, or RSAT, which is the state rehab residential program. Instead, I've decided to make the decision for you and I'm sending you to RSAT."

She crumbled to the floor as I sat there in the courtroom. Although RSAT was a rehab program, it was also known to be one of the toughest programs around, and worst of all it was located behind bars at one of the women's state prison facilities. Even if it was not in the general population, it was still in prison. I could hardly believe this was happening to my beautiful girl. My heart was crushed, and that overwhelming helpless feeling once again engulfed me.

During those times when I would ask Melanie if she was ready yet, I had often followed it up by saying "Mel, you have the opportunity to make this decision for yourself right now. If you don't decide, one day someone else is going to decide for you and then you'll have no choice." After she was sentenced The Holy Spirit brought this conversation back to my remembrance as I sat outside the courtroom, recalling the words of the judge. Strangely, even though my heart was broken a supernatural peace came over me.

Moment of Reflection: Have you ever had something bad happen to you, yet you felt peace in your heart? Isn't it such a strange feeling? What did you think it was? What did you do during this time?

CHAPTER 17

When the Alarm Bells Begin to Sound

From the time Melanie got arrested until the time she was released from the RSAT program she had been incarcerated for exactly one full year. During this year, we had some of the best and most heartfelt discussions that we had in many years. In a great sense I had my daughter back. She embraced the program and became a leader among her peers. When Melanie died I received cards, letters and messages from many of those who attended the program with her.

After her release, she came to stay with us for a couple of weeks as we had agreed living with us permanently was not the best option. In hindsight, I have often wondered if this was a mistake. Would she still be alive today if I had allowed her to live with us? The reality of it though, was that Melanie didn't want to live with her parents. She was ready to be out on her own, leading an independent life and making her own decisions.

After a couple of weeks of being home with us Melanie was invited to live in an apartment with several other women through the Sober Living of America (SLA) program. The apartment was less than 30 minutes from where we live, and it allowed us to see one another easily, attend church together and remain connected as a family. We had been rebuilding our relationship and enjoying one another's company. I was so happy and once again, so very hopeful.

I would pick Melanie up every week to go food shopping and we'd have lunch together while we were out. We started doing all the fun mother-daughter things we had missed out on over the past several years, like mani-pedis, and Melanie's favorite – shoe, clothes, and makeup shopping, though sneakers were her passion.

After a couple of months of working the program and attending classes at night she was still going strong. One day she told me about a guy she met at SLA. He lived in one of the men's apartments and according to her, "was very nice, had a good job and was working the program."

I'm certain I inwardly cringed at this remark because it was like deja vu.

The contract she signed with SLA stated they could not have any relationships while in the program, and definitely not with any of the other residents. Soon after this she and Sean began spending their weekends together. After only a couple of short months I began to sense a change in her. When she came over for Thanksgiving, she told me they had broken up. "Mom, he is not the man I thought he was. I deserve to be treated with respect. I am loyal and kind and don't deserve to be treated this way." She told me he was controlling and jealous, and although he hadn't outright hit her, he had pushed her. These words were triggers for me. I encouraged her to stay strong and not get back together with him. From my earlier years during my first marriage these two things concerned me greatly. A man who is controlling and jealous, and physically touches a woman in any way, is a recipe for disaster. Melanie was just beginning to regain her self-confidence, walked with her head held high and joy in her heart. Little by little I began to see this slowly disintegrate.

Regrettably, Melanie never got over the desperate need to be loved by a man. Although I tried to encourage her to be an independent woman this remained a focus for her all the days of her life, which I firmly believe stems from growing up without a father. She was attending church and knew who she was in the Lord and for that I was thrilled. But throughout her entire life she was continually searching for that one person who was going to love her unconditionally and accept her as she was.

After confiding in me, she knew me well enough to know I would not approve of her continuing a relationship with Sean, so when they did resume seeing one another she didn't tell me. When we were together, she began stepping away to take her incoming phone calls, but more importantly the joy she previously had in her eyes was growing dimmer. We knew one another so well that I didn't even have to say anything. She sensed my disapproval, and I just hoped she would come to her senses and that the relationship would eventually burn itself out and she would walk away.

By Christmas she started showing signs that alarmed me further. She was tired all the time, became short tempered, and began acting in a manner that I referred to as "the old Melanie." We continued to talk daily and see one another weekly. There were even a few times I sporadically dropped by to take her to lunch. I tried to get her to open up to me and tell me what was wrong as it was obvious something was. She finally told me she got back together with Sean, but things remained very inconsistent in the relationship. He was still very controlling, didn't trust her and was always calling to find out where she was and who she was with – even when she was with me. She was becoming very anxiety-ridden once again.

This behavior continued to set off alarm bells for me, but she was simply unable to walk away from the relationship.

As we rolled into the new year, she developed sciatica and was in severe pain. I was concerned that she would get pain meds to help relieve the intense pain and instead took her to the chiropractor, and provided any other natural remedies we could find to help get relief. We continued to talk multiple times a day and even though I asked her if she was taking anything, I received a resounding, "NO!"

By early February not much had changed and I had to try and get to the bottom of things because simply put, she was extremely unhappy. Gone was the smiling, carefree girl who was always laughing and looking forward to her new life. Her joy was absolutely gone. Each time I saw her she didn't appear to be high, but her attitude had changed dramatically. She went from being happy and outgoing and helping those around her to being introverted and quiet with signs of extreme anxiety. This wasn't her. On February 7th I told her I was going to pick her up and take her to lunch at a place of her choosing. She was excited as we hadn't been to lunch in two weeks. We went to a local Thai restaurant where we sat and talked and laughed. She seemed like her old self again. She said things were going well with Sean and physically she was feeling better. We shopped in the little boutiques and after a while I dropped her off at home. Although we texted and talked on the phone, that was the last time I would see my daughter alive.

Moment of Reflection: If you knew the last time you would see your loved one, would be the last time is there anything different you would do or say?

CHAPTER 18

Reflecting on the Last Days

As I reflect on that time, I can clearly see what I wasn't ready to face then. Only 5 days after our nice lunch together, when I thought everything was fine and back on track, my subsequent text messages revealed otherwise:

February 12, 2020: 4:22 p.m.

Me: After talking with you I continue to be concerned about your sobriety. I know you may think I'm naïve or just plain stupid. Or you may just think you're doing a great job of faking your way thru, but I've talked to you for years. I know what your voice sounds like when you're on something. I know the tone. The cadence. The rapid fire and the thick-tongued speech. I've heard it all and that's what I'm hearing today - 3 days shy of what would be 18 months of sobriety. But I've felt this in my gut since December. I'd rather have the truth! Just be honest and let's get back to getting help.

I didn't hear back from Melanie for 24 hours.

February 13, 2020: 5:21 p.m.

Melanie: Hey Mom! I've been asleep. I am fine. We do need to talk but tomorrow would be better! I Love You!

I knew something was not right and I wasn't about to let another day go by without talking with my girl. I wanted to wait until after I put Cameron to bed so we could speak freely. While I wasn't sure exactly what was going on, instinctively I knew it wasn't going to be good news and I didn't want him to overhear any of our conversation. Before I got a chance to call, she texted to let me know she was no longer at SLA and that she and Sean were discharged for missing curfew. Once I read that I retreated upstairs to call her privately. As a mom, I will admit, I was still in denial because I didn't want to go back there. Walking side by side with your loved one who has SUD is such a hard road. But I do believe the Holy Spirit was preparing me for this conversation.

Moments into our conversation, Melanie admitted the truth about why they were asked to leave the program and broke down, confiding in me that she had relapsed. My heart sank when I heard these words. Not for myself, even though I knew what was ahead, but for my girl. All the work she'd done in rehab and all the steps forward she had taken felt like they had slipped down into a dark abyss. I knew there was still a chance to recover, but why? Why did this happen? How is it possible we were finding ourselves back on this awful rollercoaster ride once again?

"I've come so far, Mom. I'm not going back. I refuse to give up after all I've gone through to get here." Although I felt completely devastated by this news I didn't let on. Instead, I quietly said, "Melanie, I'm not going to yell at you or give you a speech because no one feels worse about this than you do." And I honestly meant it. I could hear how broken she was. The shame emanated through the phone and pierced my heart. Oh, how I wanted to run over to that hotel and rescue her, but I knew it was something only she could do. If only getting her out of there and bringing her home with me would have fixed things I would have done so immediately. But that's not how this disease works. If love could save our children, we would not be in a place in our country where over 93,000 people have died in a 12-month period during 2020 - 2021.

I've been on this rollercoaster life of being the mom to a child with the disease of SUD for more than a decade and I've heard it all. I've gone through the myriad of emotions one can experience: happiness, anger, heartbreak, hope, sadness, great expectations, more anger, resentment, fear, concern, anxiety, disbelief, devastation, and confusion. Having a loved one with this disease provides a lifetime of living with the highest highs and the lowest of lows. On those rare times when the waters are still and the ride is steady, we are grateful as we hope and pray, this is truly the time they will be able to remain clean and sober.

Moment of Reflection: Has your life every felt like you're on a rollercoaster ride? It can be a sickening feeling. The twists and turns tearing up your insides. How can we remove ourselves from this ride and still help those we love?

CHAPTER 19

February 18 – The Prompting of the Holy Spirit

I woke up with an uneasiness in my spirit on February 18th and although this wasn't a totally unusual way for me to feel, I figured it was obviously due to Melanie's relapse. Over the years it had happened many times, but everything always worked out. That feeling which can oftentimes be an uneasiness, a heaviness or perhaps just a strong thought about someone is a good indication something is happening in that person's life. I've become attuned to when the Holy Spirit places someone on my heart. When this happens it's always a good thing to stop and lift them up in prayer. I don't know what the trouble may be, but I've learned to obey this prompting and pray. Have there been times I've totally missed it? I sure have. I can't tell you how many times I've had a person cross my mind, and I'll just be going along on my merry way when I think of them and wonder how they are. Only later I would find out they had been sick or had some challenge in their life and needed prayer. My friends, this is how the Holy Spirit and the gift of discernment works. When this happens, I try to lift up a prayer, no matter how small. Even Melanie knew this.

After she ran ahead to heaven I was going through some of her papers one day and I found an essay she wrote for one of her classes in RSAT: *"The person I admire the most in my life would be my* mother. *Without a shadow of a doubt! She has been my biggest cheer-leader, my rock, and has never left my side. Even in my darkest hour. She has always been there. She has such discernment, that when I am having a bad day or something bad has happened, or about to happen, she always knows. She feels it in her spirit."* Which is why I have asked myself numerous times, "Why didn't I do something more when I woke up feeling this way on February 18th?" I know I was busy and preoccupied with getting everything ready for our trip, but why didn't I do more than call and text? Perhaps somewhere deep inside I didn't want to deal with it right then. I wanted to get on that plane and head into the sunshine and warmth. But then I remind myself, nothing takes God by surprise.

After arriving at the airport, the uneasiness continued to stir in my spirit. I tried to call Melanie but to no avail. When we landed in Naples I texted, and a few hours later as we ate dinner I stepped away and tried to call and text again. While there had been times when she would be sleeping it off, we always connected at some point. It was rare when more than 24 hours would pass by without any word from her, even if it was a result of me Facebook stalking her. If I saw her online I'd quickly send a message, and she would always respond. Although we had just talked the night before, and put together a plan for her to go to a detox so she could return to the program, I hadn't spoken to her since then. The uneasiness in my spirit wouldn't ease up.

At 11:24 p.m. I called and texted her one more time, but no response.

Moment of Reflection: The Bible says that God knows the end from the beginning, which means nothing takes him by surprise. Was the Holy Spirit trying to warn me of what was to come? Has something like this ever happened to you?

CHAPTER 20

Running Ahead to Heaven

The moment my eyes opened on February 19 at 6:40 a.m. I immediately picked up the phone from the nightstand and called Melanie. The phone rang and rang ultimately going to voice mail. Now I was really getting worried.

The friends we were staying with had no idea about this recent turn of events. Melanie had been doing so well and I wasn't ready to let anyone know she had relapsed. This is a prime example of the stigma that surrounds the disease of addiction. It is so heavy and causes us to feel a sense of shame, even though we have nothing to be ashamed of!

My girlfriend and I had an appointment at the spa that morning. It was a belated birthday gift for me, and although we had been looking forward to it, I could not enjoy myself. Laying there as I got a facial all I could think of was Melanie. The moment it was over I hopped off the table and practically ran into the dressing room to retrieve my phone and see if she had called. Nothing!

As I was sitting there wondering what to do my phone rang. It was a friend of Melanie's who wanted to know if I'd heard from her as he hadn't been able to reach her since Monday night, which was around the same time I had last spoken with her. He had called her several times the day before and even called the hotel at 1:00 a.m. and asked the staff if they would check on her.

I texted Melanie one more time and told her if she didn't answer me within 30 minutes I would send the police for a well check visit. She never wanted anything to do with the police so I figured if nothing else this would scare her, and she would call me back immediately. I also called the front desk of the hotel, but no one answered.

At this point, I called Melanie's friend back explaining that I was in Florida and asked if he would drive to the hotel and check on her in person since we couldn't reach anyone. He agreed to do this for me and said he would call me the moment he arrived.

By this time my girlfriend found me in the dressing room. This was not a time for shame or hiding, and I quickly explained what was happening, telling her I thought something was wrong with Melanie and we had to leave right away. We quickly dressed and as we were driving back to her house my phone rang, "Mrs. Pat I just pulled up to the hotel and the Crime Scene Unit is here along with a lot of police." My heart sank in a way I had not known was possible. How I continued to drive is beyond me, but it was like being on autopilot. As he began freaking out, in a stern voice that came out of nowhere, I calmly but firmly told him to get out of his car and approach the first officer he could find and give him the phone.

I wish I could say it was a blur from this moment on, but instead I remember every detail. It's a time in my life I will never forget. So surreal, and similar to what I would imagine an out of body experience may be like – viewing this as someone else from above.

When the officer took the phone, I identified myself and asked what was happening there. I explained to him that my daughter had been staying at the hotel and I had not been able to reach her for over 24 hours. From that point forward the phone was passed around between three detectives as they each asked me a series of questions. I remained on the line during this entire time as each one said they couldn't tell me anything yet. I'm sure I sounded desperate because at one point I pleaded with the detective to tell me if my daughter was there or not. His response was, "Ma'am I wish I could tell you but due to the positioning of the body we are unable to confirm anything at this time." It was my first indication whoever they found had died since he referred to "a body." As he said those words I was still in denial. Yes, someone had died, but certainly it was not my daughter. This is something that you read about in the newspaper, and something that happens to other people. This couldn't be happening to our family! This could not be happening to me!

While the situation continued to unfold, I was still clinging to the hope this was not my girl. As I held on to the phone waiting for news, I decided to pull up the records for Melanie's phone. She never went anywhere without it and I figured I'd be able to see when she used it last. If it was used recently then I would know it wasn't her in the hotel.

I was finally able to locate the information and what I saw seemed unbelievable to me. My eyes scanned it over and over a few times to be sure I was processing it accurately. The last phone call was made was at 9:50 a.m. on Tuesday, February 18th – more than 24 hours before! It didn't register to me then, but later I would come to realize Melanie's last phone call was also the same exact time frame I had stepped into the shower at home the day before and saw my father!

Moments later, at 12:25 p.m. on Wednesday, February 19th a man whose voice I didn't recognize and wasn't one of the three I had been speaking with got on the phone. He identified himself as the Medical Examiner and asked me if I was the mother of Melanie Travassos. As I said yes, I then heard the words no mother ever wants to hear in her lifetime, "I regret to inform you that your daughter is deceased."

Moment of Reflection: Have you had a nightmare come true experience? Where do you turn? How do you process things when life's toughest moments come crashing down?

CHAPTER 21

The Long Return Home

We were in Florida for less than 24 hours before we had to fly back home. We didn't tell Cameron about Melanie's death until we were safely home as I didn't know how he would handle the news and we still had a long day ahead of us as we traveled.

Once we arrived home there was no more putting off the one thing I absolutely dreaded doing. We had to break our little boy's heart with news no young child should have to hear. God's gentle grace and mercy covered us all during those moments, as Cameron clung onto me until he finally fell asleep.

As I left him sleeping in our bed, I crept downstairs where I could finally have a few moments to myself. It was an excruciatingly long 9 hours later when I could finally be alone, let go and cry my heart out over the loss of my daughter. As we traveled home, in my effort to protect Cameron, I felt I had to remain strong and stifle all my emotions.

When I finally went back upstairs and climbed into bed, I never slept, but instead sat straight up in the bed, staring off into the darkness, numb and in utter disbelief. At 4:00 a.m. I finally went back downstairs and made coffee. As I stumbled around the kitchen I began talking to the Lord, asking him why. *"Why did this*

*happen now, Father? Why, when she'd come so far? You spared her
life so many times before, why not this time?"*

Then, it hit me - out of nowhere! Like a lightbulb exploding
in my mind. Suddenly, I remembered seeing my father about 42
hours earlier! As I stepped into that steamy shower, there he was,
standing there dressed all in white, in the shirt with the tiny brown
buttons. My dad, looking so very young and handsome.

How could I have forgotten something like that? How is that
even possible? Yet, it only took a matter of seconds for it all to come
tumbling back, as I remembered seeing the vision of my father after
stepping into the shower just the morning before. Then, two very
important facts immediately came flooding to the forefront of my
mind almost simultaneously – the time I stepped into the shower
on February 18 was 9:45 a.m. and Melanie's last phone call was at
9:50 a.m. In that moment, I knew beyond a shadow of a doubt, God
assigned my Dad one more mission – he came to escort my girl
home safely to heaven.

My Dad had been a veteran of World War II and like many
who fought in that war, he saw a lot of combat and had experienced horrific things. When he returned home he began drinking
as a way to forget all he had seen and done. He was a kind, loving
father who worked hard to support our family, but he also battled
the disease of addiction, just like Melanie, except instead of drugs
he chose alcohol.

As I began to recall that encounter with my Dad, it was in
the initial moments after I realized I was seeing my dead father,
I thought I was the one who may be dying, and he was coming to
take me home. Now it was all coming together and began to make
sense to me now. It wasn't me he was coming for after all. It was
my beautiful girl, and the Lord allowed my Dad to accompany her

home. But in only God's infinite and mighty way, by allowing me to see my Dad, it gave me a small sense of comfort knowing she was escorted to heaven by her Grandpa, but it also answered a question that had haunted me since he died.

I never knew if my Dad had gone to heaven. When he was alive we tried to talk with him about the Lord, but he always said he had done some things he didn't think could be forgiven. This moment of seeing my Dad not only confirmed to me that he was in heaven, but I had the reassurance that with Melanie's last breath Jesus allowed my Dad to surround my girl with comfort and protection as he escorted her home to heaven. Oh, Jesus, how great and merciful you are.

As this all came together in my kitchen during the wee hours of the morning, and even in the midst of my shock, sadness, and utter disbelief that my daughter was no longer on this earth, I stood in awe and wonderment of how truly great our God is.

Heavenly Father, thank you for the gift of your son Jesus. Thank you for loving us so much you sent him as a sacrifice for us so that we may live forever with you in heaven. This journey has made the words of Psalm 23 more real to me than ever before because yes, even though I am walking through the valley of the shadow of death, you are with me. You make me lie down in green pastures and you restore my soul. Even during the grief and sorrow of missing my girl, I will not turn from you. The enemy thought he won the day Melanie took her last breath, but he didn't. Thank you for rescuing my girl and although I will miss her all the days of my life, I look forward to the day I will see her again.

Part Two:
The Grief Journey

"The Lord is close to the brokenhearted and
saves those who are crushed in spirit"

Psalm 34:18

"Blessed are those who mourn for
they shall be comforted"

Matthew 5:4

"I don't believe we ever actually recover from grief;
we simply learn how to live our lives the best we
can around the missing piece of our heart."

~ Pat Elsberry

CHAPTER 22

Grief is a Lonely Walk

As time went by the reality of Melanie's death started to really hit home for me. The days turned into weeks, then weeks into months and it seemed as if everyone's life was moving forward without so much as a backward glance. This is when the grief journey truly began for me and I realized we each take the path alone.

Although I have family and well-meaning friends who would call or text to check on me, that feeling of isolation settled deep into my heart. When I did talk with people what I soon noticed was an awkwardness surrounding the conversation. It's like the proverbial elephant in the room. Most people didn't dare broach the subject that my daughter had recently died, or some didn't even ask how I was doing for fear of my answer. Every subject imaginable was broached, but most didn't dare go where I longed for them to be. They asked about everything except the one thing that consumed me – the state of my heart and the overwhelming sadness over the loss of my girl!

As time slipped by Melanie's name would rarely be mentioned, as if she never existed. It was as though life had just gone back to normal, and for them, it had. For me, I had barely begun walking that long road back to whatever my new normal might be. The grief journey is a long, slow, twisting road we are forced to travel on. I had barely left the garage, yet everyone else was traveling down the highway at 80 mph and expecting me to be the same person I was before.

Loneliness was not a feeling I was familiar with and when you experience a traumatic, unexpected, or out of order death the journey can be a very solitary road. Now, this isn't a woe-is-me statement, it's just reality. When you're grieving the loss of a loved one, it's hard to understand unless you've been there. Before Melanie died, I thought I understood grief and loss. I thought I was sympathetic and supportive, and I was, but I've discovered how little I really knew, or how complex grief can be. It's such a personal journey and is so very different for each of us. Even with a great support system there is no one on this earth who can fill the void and erase the hurt that comes from the loss of your loved one.

One afternoon I was sitting outside trying to let the warmth of the sun seep inside what felt cold and dead inside of me. I didn't know how I was going to fill the void that was left behind by no longer having my daughter on this earth. So, I did the one thing I knew I could do and that was cry out to God. No matter what's happened in my life I knew he would be there for me and would never leave me alone.

Did you know that praying is just simply having a conversation with God? You don't need eloquent words; you just need to share your heart. And that was what I did that day as I sat outside with my Heavenly Father, who already knew what I was feeling before I even spoke the words aloud.

In the middle of my tears, I remembered one of God's promises, *"I'll never let you down, never walk off and leave you" (Hebrews*

13:5 MSG). This promise applies to me and you. Although we may feel lonely, we are truly never alone.

Moment of Reflection: How does God speak to you in the everyday?

CHAPTER 23

Eye of the Storm

God continues to use music to speak to my heart. I've become accustomed to receiving these songs in the night. Interestingly, it's always just a few lines that repeat over and over in my head until I either get up and write them down or tap a few words into my phone. There are certainly some nights I want to throw the pillow over my head and shout, "Just let me sleep, Lord!"

For some reason since Melanie's death, I have been awakened with these songs in the night more than ever before. I don't understand it, nor can I rationalize it, but I also realize *"His ways are not our ways." Isaiah 55:8-9* Perhaps God knew I need more encouragement now than I ever have and this is one of the ways the Holy Spirit encourages and comforts me. And in case you're wondering, these are not songs I've recently heard on the radio or just listened to before going to bed. That's one of the amazing things! God loves his children so much that he gives us songs in the night to lift us up as we walk this dark, lonely journey of grief.

I think of my girl the moment my eyes open, and she's the last thing I think of before I go to sleep at night. I picture in my mind what it must have been like when she took her last breath on earth and then imagine what it must have been like when her next breath was in heaven, looking at Jesus. Yes, I can only imagine!

The day after Melanie died, I was talking with a friend on the phone. What I remember most about the conversation was that from out of nowhere a holy anger rose up within me as I told him, "The enemy thought he won last night when Melanie took her last breath but, I'm here to tell you he didn't win at all! I know that Melanie is in heaven with Jesus!"

Melanie and I had many conversations about the Lord over the years. She would tell me she wasn't religious – she was spiritual. One day during one of the very darkest times of her addiction, she was homeless and living on the street. As we spoke on the phone, I asked her directly, "Melanie Anne, if you died today do you know where you'd go?" With a little bit of a laugh, she quickly and confidently replied, "Yes, momma, I know exactly where I'm going! Just because I'm an addict doesn't mean that I don't love Jesus and believe in him!!" Ha! Well, that sure gave me something to think about! Just because someone is struggling with the disease of addiction doesn't mean they don't have a relationship with God, nor have they abandoned their faith.

No one ever dreams of becoming an addict or having the disease of addiction. Melanie hated this about herself. She didn't understand why she couldn't overcome it. Why couldn't she walk away? Why couldn't she quell the cravings that would eventually consume her? I can't count how many times she cried out, "I just want to be normal and live a normal life." Her heart wanted this, but the disease that controlled the brain would overtake her heart's greatest desire.

I do take some comfort in the fact that her struggle is over. Me? As her momma I will always miss her voice, her smile, our daily talks, our early morning, and nightly texts – about nothing and everything. It's in the eye of this storm, where I will continue to rely on the only one who can calm the storm within me.

Moment of Reflection: When you feel as if you're in the eye of a storm, what is your first instinct?

CHAPTER 24

The Big "A" – Anxiety

F
ear. Anxiety. Worry. Ever since Melanie died these words have become my new reality. When Cameron drops something behind me that I wasn't expecting I jump like a bomb just went off. As my husband is taking the garbage out and it unexpectedly bangs against the door, I practically come out of my own skin. When did this happen? How did it happen?

I know many who struggle with anxiety. It's nothing to be ashamed of. I fought and won this battle decades ago and now, here it is. Back again. Knocking at my door. The thing is, I don't want to walk in fear, wondering what the next bad thing is that's going to blow up my life. But apparently, this is common when walking through grief.

When your child dies and you hear those words, it's not something that simply just goes away. The images in your mind are not so easily erased. I believe when an unexpected and tragic death occurs, the negative thoughts and feelings that suddenly seem to pummel you from every direction are quite normal.

During the first several months after Melanie died, fear and anxiety even gripped my sweet boy. Every time I would get ready to leave the house he would ask, "Where are you going? What time will you be back? How long will you be gone?" When Fred would run out to do an errand, if he seemed to take longer than Cameron expected he wanted to know what was taking him so long. There it is again. Knock, knock, knocking on my door. Fear. Anxiety. Worry. You are not welcome here!

It's important for us as parents to recognize this in our children so we can provide them with the comfort and the security needed to ensure everything is okay.

Fear and trust were two things Melanie continually struggled with. Fear of the future. Fear of people. Fear of failure. Fear of getting high. Fear of not getting high. Fear of not being loved. Fear of not being enough. Fear of not being accepted. She often said she didn't trust anyone, but in her everyday battle, she did trust, just all the wrong people. This was something we even talked about the day before she died.

During our last phone call, she had an epiphany and with a very sad voice said, "Mom, you were right. I really am a very bad judge of character." I didn't want to be right, but I also couldn't argue with her. It was true. Unfortunately, it was, in part, due to placing her trust in the wrong people that she is no longer with us today.

When we cry out to the Lord, he hears us (Psalm 18:6), and he will answer us in many ways. God's words are the weapons of our warfare. This has become my battle cry! If I'm in a war for my soul, my mind, my peace, I'm going to fight it on my knees and with everything I have in me.

Music is one of the ways God continually ministers to my hurting heart, using the words like a balm to my soul. It brings peace in the middle of the wreckage, and is a sweet and gentle reminder I don't have to fear. I don't have to worry.

Have I won the battle? Not entirely, but I'm fighting it every step of the way. I'm determined that each day I'm closer to winning the war and I will remember, "I will trust you Lord. I will fear no more."

Melanie understood anxiety and she wouldn't want me or Cameron to become paralyzed with it. This is yet another reason to rise up and say: *"God has not given me a spirit of fear, but of love, power and a sound mind" (2 Timothy 1:7).*

Moment of Reflection: Have you waged war against fear or anxiety? What do you do to regain your sense of peace?

CHAPTER 25

See the Light

During the summer months one of the things I like most is how it stays light outside until late in the evening. There is something about the warmth and beauty of the summer days that brings a warmth and peace to my soul. As a young girl growing up outside of Boston, summers were short. As soon as Labor Day rolled around, not only would you stop wearing white, but the weather also changed and you were soon digging out a light jacket, as the weather began to get a little bit cooler. Now that I'm living in the South, I love that we can stretch out the warmth of those summer days until at least early November. But no matter where I've lived, or how long or short the summer months are I'll admit there has always been something about the light that draws me in and fills me with peace.

Recently, the words to the song, *See the Light*, began coming up in my heart repeatedly. The song was written by one of Cameron's favorite Christian artists, Toby Mac. I had never heard of Toby until about 5 years ago when my then 7-year-old introduced me to his music. I've since become a fan myself.

Little did I know then how similar my life as a suburban mom would parallel with a Christian artist from Tennessee. What I didn't know, and what the world at large wasn't aware of, was that Toby's oldest son, Truett was fighting the same disease as Melanie.

You see, it really doesn't matter where you come from. Whether you're famous or the family next door. A single parent or married for 25 years to your high school sweetheart. Rich, poor, living in the best neighborhood or living in the projects. In the church, or out of the church – Substance Use Disorder doesn't discriminate or care about those things! This disease touches people from all walks of life.

Back in October 2019, I remember reading a post on Toby's social media asking the public to pray for him and his family as Truett had died at the age of 21. The cause of Truett's death wasn't immediately publicized and quite frankly, the reason for his death wasn't what was most important. A mother and father just lost their firstborn at a very young age. Death and grief touch at the core of our heart whether it's a child, spouse, parent, sibling, or close friend. Whether they've died from a car accident, disease, or any other myriad of reasons, the pain and hurt are all the same. Grief is grief. Sadness is sadness. Loss is loss. What remains most memorable to me was the statement Toby shared (my paraphrase): *"God is still our rock, no matter what the circumstances and we will continue to love and serve him."*

I've thought more about heaven now than I ever have and I've often wondered what it was like when Melanie saw the light of our Lord and Savior, Jesus Christ. As I listen to the words of this song by my brother in Christ, it brings a whole new meaning to me today.

In many ways we are all connected. We live in a broken world and sometimes bad things do happen to good people. God never promised us a trouble-free life. Instead, he promised that *"he would never leave us nor forsake us"* (Deuteronomy 31:8). *"He would be with us as we pass through deep waters and when you walk through the fire you will not be burned"* (Isaiah 43:2). No matter what, during this uphill climb, we need to cling to the One who can take us through it all.

Moment of Reflection: Have you ever heard the saying, light shines brightest in the dark? When things looked so dark and bleak, but then something happened, and you realized it was God opening a window in what may have appeared to be a closed room. Have you ever had a moment like this?

CHAPTER 26

Healing Comes in Many Ways

The Christmas before Melanie died I found myself listening to the Celebration of Life service for Lois Evans, wife of
Dr. Tony Evans and mother of well-known Christian author and
speaker, Priscilla Shirer. At the time I couldn't say why I decided
to listen to this, but in hindsight I believe God drew me there.

I certainly enjoy listening to Priscilla and her powerful
messages aimed toward encouraging women in their walk with
Christ, but I can't explain why I felt drawn to listen to her mother's
funeral service. I learned of Lois' cancer diagnosis several months
earlier and knew the family had been believing God for a miracu-
lous healing.

One of Lois' sons spoke at the service and shared something
that sticks in my mind until this day. He told the story about the
day his mom shared with the family that she had cancer, and all
the things they did both medically and prayerfully to believe for
her healing. Then he said, "Momma was either going to be healed,
OR she was going to be healed"! As it would be, Lois was healed – it
just didn't happen on this side of heaven. When I first listened to
that service, I had no idea that just a few short months later I would
be burying my own 38-year-old daughter. But God knew.

I look back on this now and I see how He was preparing me for
what was about to happen. He is The Alpha and The Omega – the

beginning and the end. Just like Lois Evans, Melanie was healed. It sure wasn't in the way I had expected, but when I think about my girl, I feel a total peace in my heart knowing she is free! Free from the constant struggle and heaviness that the weight of addiction brought to her for so long. It doesn't eliminate the sadness that I feel on those days when I'm missing her terribly. I'll always miss hearing her voice on the other end of my phone or looking into those beautiful light brown eyes and seeing her pretty, but sometimes, mischievous smile. As each day unfolds, whatever it brings, I will continue to go to my rock and place all my tears and cares there.

Moment of Reflection: Have you ever had a situation like this in your life? Have you prayed for healing, or something else, and it was manifested in a way you didn't expect?

CHAPTER 27

The Blanket of Love

My mother taught me how to crochet when I was 8 years old. It was something we did together, especially during those long, winter days. We crocheted everything and anything – scarves, mittens, vests, skirts! My mom, along with my Aunt Martha would crochet around the edge of these special handkerchiefs, some of which I still happen to have today. I even crocheted a purple vest for my big crush and love of my 12 year old life, Donny Osmond! Oh, my sweet momma helped me box it up in pretty purple tissue paper, which we then carefully wrapped in a brown paper bag, before taking it to the post office to mail to his home in Provo, UT. Gee, I wonder what happened to that vest when it arrived?!

When I was pregnant with each of my children, I crocheted their first baby blanket. Each one made with so much love. I still have them both today and had hoped to pass them down to their children. John doesn't have any kids yet so his is still packed away and when Melanie had Cameron, well, I knew he wouldn't want a pink blanket, so I made him one.

When John and Melanie got older and moved out on their own, I would eventually crochet each of them a blanket to fit their bed. Now if you know anything about crocheting, you understand that making a small baby blanket versus a king size one is a much bigger time commitment. It's days and weeks of time vs. hours, but it was something special that I longed to do for them. In my mind, it was a tangible item they could have forever, and when I was no longer here maybe they would wrap themselves in it and remember my love that came along with each stitch.

Due to Melanie's addiction, she didn't spend many Christmases with us for about 7 years. But what a blessing it was that we were able to be together as a family during her last Christmas here.

In late November I decided I would make Melanie a new blanket for her bed. I began working on it each night and in every free moment I had. I started stressing over whether I'd be finished in time and wondered why I did this to myself. Why didn't I come up with these great ideas earlier in the year and not in the middle of the crunch of the holidays? But truly, I loved every moment of making it and couldn't wait to see her face when she opened this special gift. It was two days before Christmas when I finally completed it. As I laid my hands on it I prayed that each time Melanie placed that blanket on top of her she would be reminded of how much I loved her, and that she would know and feel the love of her Heavenly Father. I couldn't always be with her, but I prayed the Holy Spirit would envelop her with love, courage, and strength to keep walking in his light.

No matter how old Melanie was, when Christmas rolled around she behaved like a little kid. She was always the one who counted all the gifts making sure it was even! She was also the one who shook each box to guess what was inside. I found out years later there was one Christmas she and John opened each gift while I was at work and then taped them all back up! She was certainly the mischief maker in the family!

On this Christmas morning, she couldn't figure out what could possibly be in this big box! She saved it until the end to open it and

I can still see the look on her face when she realized what it was – her very own, blanket of love! I had always told them I called it a blanket of love because each and every stitch was made with all the love in my heart for them.

With tears in her eyes and a special look between just the two of us, we understood the meaning behind this gift. You see, I had made Melanie a blanket of love years before but somewhere along her hard road, she lost it. For my girl, this beautiful pink blanket was a symbol. A new start. A new beginning. She had her family back and the unconditional love of her mother, staring back at her with every loving stitch.

When Melanie died and I received her things the first thing I saw was her blanket of love poking out of the bag. I immediately pulled it out and held it close to my face. It smelled just like her! In the early days after she was gone, I would keep it next to me and reach over and just breathe in her scent. It made me feel as if she was still here with me. I have since folded it up and have it on a chair in my bedroom and many nights before I climb into bed, I lean my face down into her blanket of love and just breathe.

Recently, I began thinking about how much comfort that blanket brings to me. Even when I just look over at it, it's like a small piece of her remains here with me. Her perfume still lingering on the wool. Then, I begin thinking about how much more our Heavenly Father loves us and wants to wrap us in His arms, bringing us comfort. His love covers us like the warmest and softest blanket of all. *He shelters us from the storms of life, comforting us and keeping us from harm. (Psalm 91).*

On the days when I am struggling, I'll lay my head and heart at the feet of my Heavenly Father as I walk through the valley and be thankful that *His mercies are new every morning (Lamentations 3:22-23).*

Moment of Reflection: Do you have an item of your loved ones that you have kept close to you during this journey?

CHAPTER 28

Back to the Classroom: Grief 101

W hen I was growing up, I loved school and I especially loved getting ready for the new year. My mom and I would take the train into Downtown Boston and go shopping at Filene's Basement and Jordan Marsh. We made a day of it and after shopping we would then walk over to Chinatown to eat the best Chinese food my lips ever tasted. I remember rubbing the belly of the Buddha as we entered sending up a wish for a great school year.

Though our preparations for school today are completely different, memories flood my mind of days gone by. Even when John and Melanie were little, I loved the whole process of getting them ready for school: shopping for new clothes, shoes, backpacks that would then be filled with colored folders and new pencils. So much has changed from those days. Today I'm buying a laptop, a desk, and a chair to outfit a digital learning environment to support learning both at home and in school. Yet, the excitement of it all still rumbles underneath.

When John and Melanie were in elementary school I remember one day when I picked them up, Melanie's teacher leaned into the car and said, "Melanie is so sweet. She's such a social child!" Oh, no! I knew what that meant! That was code for, "Melanie talks all the time and isn't concentrating on her schoolwork!" As the years went by, some things never changed. She made friends wherever she went, always had a sparkle in her eye, and was always smiling and giggling while she continued to talk non-stop. I have a treasured school photo of Melanie when she was about 6 years old, showing off her beautiful smile, minus a recently lost tooth!

Since Melanie died, I have found myself back in the classroom. The main subject - "Lessons of Life and Death." I'll admit I don't particularly like these lessons very much. This type of learning isn't what I would have chosen for myself. But, unfortunately, I wasn't given a choice. Even though we all walk through life, learning as we go, I wasn't prepared for some of the lessons I've had to learn.

How do you manage through the anxiety and fear that accompanies grief? I didn't know these two things oftentimes go together when you're grieving, and I think it's been one of the toughest lessons for me.

Quite frankly, I wish I could have a more carefree attitude about some things like Melanie did. I would love to just be enjoying life, laughing, smiling, and chatting with my girlfriends over a glass of chardonnay, with not a care in the world. Instead, each day I'm sitting on the front row of class, learning about the lessons of life, death and grief.

Fear. Yes, that's on the list of topics we're covering. I have found that I am a reluctant student! I don't like this class. I don't want to talk about the fact that I'm afraid something is going to happen to another one of my family members. I don't want everyone to know the moment anyone leaves the house I wonder if they will return. I don't want to come to the realization that bad things do happen to good people and there is nothing I can do about it. I hate fear. But I think what I hate most is the feeling of not being in control of what can happen in my life.

My head tells me one thing and my heart another. My mind and spirit scream out, "Fear, you are a liar! I have not been given a spirit of fear but of love, power and a sound mind." I know this scripture intimately. After my dad died, I became filled with a spirit of fear and battled it for years. Now, it's back, haunting me and trying to tell me things I don't want to hear.

The enemy wants to keep us prisoner to our fears. However, have you ever noticed that the thing you resist most, once confronted loses its power? As hard as it is being back in the classroom, I have come to discover that fear is a natural response when an unexpected traumatic event occurs. Sometimes fear can even evolve into PTSD.

When you were a little kid were you ever afraid of the dark? I was. I found out as soon as I had the courage to step out, run into the dark room and turn the light on, there was nothing in that room that could hurt me. The fears we face today can be confronted in the same way. The mind is the battlefield, and the enemy wants to hold us hostage and keep us in the dark and afraid. Jesus is the light of my life. *In Him I am finding my weakness made strong (2 Cor 12:9).* I may even take a step backward, but it's okay. I will continue moving forward, letting *His word be a lamp to my feet and a light to my path. (Psalm 119:105)*

Moment of Reflection: What do you do to combat fear? Have you found anxiety accompanies the fear?

CHAPTER 29

In the Blink of an Eye

For those walking the grief journey if someone asked how long it had been since your loved one died you would probably be able to tell them down to the minute exactly how many days, weeks, or months it was.

When Melanie first ran ahead to heaven I counted down each day as it unfolded into weeks, and then months. The closer it came to the 6 months mark I started thinking about the adage, *What a difference a day makes.* Melanie had been gone 180 days. When the time was calculated into days it seemed like such a short time, and the realization of how quickly life can change hit me squarely between the eyes. So many things changed during those first 6 months - some good and some bad.

Time is a funny thing. So much in life can change in the blink of an eye. I've learned that 6 months can seem like yesterday, yet it can seem like decades, too. I've learned that I can be fine one moment and in tears the next. I've learned I can go days without crying, and then sob without provocation all day long. I've learned that God's peace and mercy is truly new every single morning. I've learned that the average person is very uncomfortable talking about grief and reluctant to mention the person who died by name. I've learned that those who are closest to you relationally may also not be the ones to offer the support you need. But most importantly, I've learned to have great compassion because I realize that although I am loved, some don't know what to say or do to ease the pain death brings.

Over the years of my professional career, I've taken several personality assessments. My Myers-Briggs, Strength Finder and Enneagram results have a common thread. In their own individual way, they conclude that I'm a Fixer. A problem solver. A Helper. Responsibility, Achiever, Discipline, Relator, and Empathy are my top 5-character traits. When I'm unable to achieve my results, find a solution, fix things, or help someone I'm beyond frustrated. So, I've learned to look at this grief walk from that perspective as well. I'm sure there are countless family and friends who have some of the same characteristics that I do. If they are fixers, they may look at the loss of your loved one as a very uncomfortable situation and simply think, there's nothing they can do to fix you or the situation so instead of coming closer, they draw away.

There are many reasons why our friends may abandon us in our greatest time of need. Now that I'm on this side of grief, I don't like feeling abandoned but I'm learning that when life changes in the blink of an eye it can scare people. If something like an unexpected death can happen to me, then maybe it can happen to them, too. And that is scary, so they run in the other direction.

Perhaps another reason they stop being supportive is because we are taking too long sitting in our grief. When we continue to grieve, it makes people very uncomfortable. Some may feel we have had enough time and should get on with our lives. I don't believe one ever realizes how insensitive and unrealistic this is until they have walked this road themselves.

One moment in February I was jetting off for a lovely vacation and in the next moment I was on the phone with a detective waiting to be told my daughter had died. Yes, life can change in the blink of an eye. So, I'm continuing to learn to take each day as it comes and embrace both my tears and the laughter. Around the 6-month mark, my heart no longer jumped out of my chest when my phone rang as it used to do when my girl was here. I no longer peruse Facebook just to see if she is online to determine if she was still breathing or not. I'm no longer calling hospitals or checking with the local police. These types of stressors are the things I don't miss. Yes, I know I will see her again one day and that she is at peace, but I will never, ever, stop missing her and wishing things could have been different.

Moment of Reflection: Have you ever felt abandoned by someone who you thought would be there to support you? What did you do?

CHAPTER 30

A T.A.P. Life

As a parent we only want the very best for our children, don't we? Although I miss Melanie so very much, I am confident she is truly in the best place she could ever be in. Does it help me to know she is in heaven living healed and whole? Absolutely. When I think solely of her well-being and the life she now has, I inwardly sigh, as my shoulders hunch over slightly and tell myself, "She is now living a totally, amazing, peaceful life." It's what I refer to as the T.A.P. Life: Total, Amazing, Peaceful. This is something that evaded Melanie, especially during the last 10 years of her young life. The disease of addiction stole that carefree part of her that I loved so much.

Today she is walking in total freedom, with amazing peace, and free from the struggle of the insidious disease of addiction. Even though as her mom, I miss her in ways that oftentimes are indescribable, how can I object to that?

I recently came across a few voicemails from her that I downloaded years ago and forgot about. What priceless gifts! I also discovered treasured letters, emails and journals which are filled with both sadness and joy, hardship and love. The many faces of Melanie all rolled up into one.

The push and pull within my heart begin again until I am reminded of T.A.P. She is Totally, Amazingly Peaceful right now and I will see her again one day. I miss my girl immensely and there is a hole in my heart that will never be filled.

My mom always said, "God works in mysterious ways" and I believe that is so true. He has taken one of the worse things to happen in my life and shined light into this darkness. Even the worst experiences in our lives will not destroy us – at least not forever. I'm learning it's possible to both smile and grieve. To laugh yet still feel sadness. These are all signs of life and living. The tears and sadness are outward signs of all the love we will continue to carry in our heart for our loved one. The only way I know how to get up, putting one foot in front of the other, is by continuing to lean toward the only one who can pick me up when I'm down. Jesus. *He heals our broken hearts and crushed spirits (Psalm 34:18).*

Moment of Reflection: Does it help to think of your loved one living a T.A.P. life?

CHAPTER 31

The Roller Coaster
Ride Called Grief

When I was a teenager, I remember how exciting it was when I got to visit Whalom Park, which was the 13th oldest amusement park in the U.S. The moment we would get there my best friend Patty and I would race over to the Flying Comet to stand in the long line waiting our turn. Once we got strapped in the seat we began the slow ascent up, up, up listening to the clickety-clack of the wooden tracks cracking and popping as we made our way up toward the sky. Our hearts would begin racing in anticipation of what lay ahead. Finally, we would reach the top and for a split second we would see the beautiful lake in front of us before we plunged down the track headfirst, hands in the air screaming at the top of our lungs! So fun and exhilarating, with a little bit of scary at the same time! When we reached the bottom, we would turn right around and head back to the line to do it all over again.

Since Melanie went to heaven my life often feels like the younger me on the Flying Comet. One day I'm cruising along, with the sun shining brightly overhead, a gentle breeze blowing in the wind, and a peaceful spirit within. In the very next moment, out of nowhere, I feel like I'm being frantically whipped around the corner, hanging off the edge of my seat as I take a curve being jerked from side to side. My heart begins pounding in my chest and for no apparent reason my old "friend" anxiety begins to seep in. Instead of the clickety-clack of the wooden tracks, all I hear is my own heart beating wildly within. I'm on a rollercoaster alright, but not the Flying Comet.

I now refer to my life in two different segments of time: BMD, Before Melanie Died and AMD, After Melanie Died. Have you found yourself beginning sentences with the statement, "Before (insert your loved one's name) died I used to (fill in the blank)? Or "Before my (daughter, son, husband, wife, sister, brother) died I never _____?" I do. I have found myself referring back to Melanie's death as a point of time that changed everything about my life. It's the rollercoaster of my AMD life.

I don't know where you are on your grief journey, but whether it's days, months, or years I believe being on this rollercoaster is actually a very normal process of moving through grief. I'm discovering what's most important for our health and wellbeing is what we do with these rollercoaster moments that matters most.

For me, I've found a few things that help me walk this journey with more peace. Journaling each day helps me capture my thoughts and feelings as I pour it all out onto the pages. I usually do this in the early morning hours when no one else is awake yet. Yes, it means that I'm usually getting up around 5:00 a.m. but it's so worth it. Starting out my day in prayer, talking to my Heavenly Father, reading from my Bible or one of my devotionals helps set my day to begin on a positive note. The other thing that gets me down off the whirls and twirls of the rollercoaster life is music. I love all types of music but during these times I focus on songs by artists who inspire me with their worship.

If you feel as if you're on the Flying Comet and being tossed back and forth like a rag doll I hope you'll take a moment for yourself today. Order yourself a beautiful journal online. Lift a simple prayer up to heaven, lean into God and ask Him to fill your heart with His peace today. *"Then you will experience God's peace, which exceeds anything we can understand. His peace will guard your hearts and minds as you live in Christ Jesus (Philippians 4:7 NLT).*

Moment of Reflection: What do you do to encourage yourself when you're feeling tossed to and fro?

CHAPTER 32

The Sunflower

There is something about the sunflower that makes me happy. Its upturned face seems surrounded by joy! Maybe it's the bright yellow color, or perhaps it just reminds me of those giant yellow smiley faces that were popular in the 70's!

Melanie's favorite flower is the sunflower. I have found it interesting that since she's been gone, I see sunflowers everywhere. In the grocery store, on the side of the road and even on my social media page! One day I received a message on Facebook from someone who was conducting mini photo shoots in a sunflower field. I couldn't believe it was located less than half a mile up the road from where I've lived for years. How did I not notice this before? I'll take it as a sign of my girl smiling down on me.

Did you know that sunflowers draw their strength from the sun? On sunny days they will turn their face upward and follow the sun from east to west. As the sun sets, it will return to its normal position then start all over again the next day. I think we can all take a lesson from the sunflower. Let's turn our faces upward, toward *The Son.*

Most of us are familiar with the movie, *The Lion King.* I have found so many wonderful life lessons in this movie. One of my favorite moments is when Mufasa is showing his young son, Simba, the big, beautiful countryside in front of him. He shares with him something his own father told him, "the day will come when I will no longer be with you but I will always be there, watching over you, guiding you." He's talking about the Circle of Life and if you are a Believer, then you know that God is always there, watching over us. *We are never alone (Heb 13:5).*

At some point in our Circle of Life we will lose someone or something we love and treasure. It may be a child, a spouse, a parent, a sibling, or perhaps a best friend. There are so many kinds of loss, yet regardless of the specific relationship or set of circumstances the feelings are the same. Heartache. Sadness. Missing. Shock. Numbness. Disbelief. Anger. These are all very valid feelings we must walk through if we hope to get to the other side.

We can still so greatly miss and love what is no longer a part of this earthly life. But just because someone is not on this side of heaven doesn't mean your loved one is no longer a part of you. We can carry them in our hearts, everywhere we go. Each day the sun will rise again, and we are gifted with a new day. I would suggest that even in our sadness and grief, let us walk down this road together and lift one another up.

Each day, I'm going to strive to be more like the beautiful sunflower – leaning in and up, toward The One who lifts me and pushes me forward, knowing the Son is watching over me, guiding my every step.

Moment of Reflection: May you be like the sunflower today and lift your face up toward The Son and feel the warmth of his presence along with a peace that surpasses all understanding.

CHAPTER 33

Calling All Masketeers

Long before there was such a thing as Covid I already wore a mask every day. In fact, I established my own personal club, which I secretly nicknamed, The Masketeer Club. Although I was the only member of this chapter, I would bet there are many of you who are members of the same club, too.

For more than 10 years just as I finished applying my Bobbi Brown foundation, and just after the last brush of mascara across my eyelashes, I would carefully slip my mask on every morning. I considered myself an expert in this area.

Now this was a full-on mask, not just one covering my nose and mouth. It didn't have pretty colors or designs and was invisible to everyone else, which to me, was the best part of all. It was exactly what I needed to hide the fear, shame, hurt, disappointment, and a host of many other feelings that come with being the mother of a child with the disease of addiction.

When I looked up the definition of expert it says, *"a person who has a comprehensive and authoritative knowledge of or skill in a particular area."* Yes, that described me, and it was also something I was proud to be skilled in! As I expertly applied my mask each day I knew no one would be able to see the real me. It helped to hide the tears that were just behind my eyes, the pretty lipstick framed a smile which really held a sad, frown underneath. My mask even helped with my gait and voice tone. Inside I felt like Eeyore, dragging my tail around behind me, heaviness enveloping every fiber of my being. But with the mask in place I could go into my office each day and no one would be the wiser.

Unfortunately, the day my girl died I could no longer be a member of The Masketeer's Club. This epiphany occurred to me as I sat at my kitchen island at 4:00 a.m. writing Melanie's eulogy. When the realization hit me that I would no longer be able to hide behind my mask any longer I began to feel anxious and exposed. This was a part of me, even if just a façade. Now everyone was going to see the real me. They would see the imposter who has been walking among them.

Yet deep down inside the Holy Spirit was pushing me forward. God was leading me to write my girl's eulogy and in doing so I would need to remove my mask completely. I prayed He would give me the strength to stand up in front of everyone and share what He had placed on my heart. I'd like to share a small part of that with you, because it's about the masks we all wear in life.

"As we celebrate Melanie's life and I considered what I wanted to share with you, I realized to do so I would have to be willing to be vulnerable – which is akin to being naked before you all. Whew, now that is a scary thought on many levels! But, the naked I'm referring to is of the heart – full and total transparency. You see, every day for the past 10 years I wouldn't leave my house without putting on my mask. As time went on, I became an expert at it, applying it each morning, just like my makeup. Well, unfortunately, since we're all here in this room I guess I can't hide behind that mask any longer. The reason for wearing the mask is because Melanie had the disease of addiction. Addiction is ugly. It's raw. It has a stigma attached to it that brings about judgment, shame, and most of all misunderstanding, of you

and your loved one. I'll admit for a long time I had quite a different outlook on what addiction was. But I want you to know that first and foremost, addiction is in fact a disease. A brain disease. It's not something you can just tell someone to get over, stop using, be strong, or suck it up buttercup. It's not that easy. I found out early on that if you know someone who has the disease of cancer you would bring a meal and see what you could do to help. Not so with the disease of addiction. Addiction doesn't only affect the addict, it affects the entire family. Thankfully, this was just a piece of Melanie's life and although she struggled on and off for many years it wasn't who she was at the very core and heart of her being. She was made by God, in His image and with His heart! And that heart is who Melanie really was! She was a loving, caring daughter, sister, cousin, and friend, and most of all, she loved Cameron with her whole being."

Sharing this very personal part of my life was scary, but also very freeing! There is so much that comes with having a loved one who battles the disease of addiction – isolation, fear, anger, hurt, and anxiety, just to name a few. We have been bound by these things for so long and I believe that if they could, our loved ones would encourage us to walk a life of freedom, which will in turn lead to peace.

The day I delivered this I stood in front of more than 125 people. A great majority of these were my co-workers and it was that group who I wore my mask for daily. After the service, and in the weeks following I had several people tell me how removing my mask had given them the courage to remove their own as they began sharing their own stories. I hope by sharing this with you now, you will also take the step and remove your own mask today.

Moment of Reflection: Are you wearing a mask today?

CHAPTER 34

Ready or Not

In the year of "firsts" as the holidays began to creep closer, I couldn't stop thinking about them and how it would be not having Melanie with us. During the early Fall I was already being inundated by thoughts of Thanksgiving and Christmas. Under normal circumstances this would not be entirely unusual for me. I'm a planner. I'm one of those people who typically buys Christmas presents throughout the year so I can have all my shopping completed before Thanksgiving. But, this was not going to be a normal year for me.

The year before Melanie died she was walking strong in her sobriety and for the first time in 7 years we were able to celebrate both Thanksgiving and Christmas together as a family. We cooked all the family favorites, including baking my mom's Italian Anise cookies and pizzelles. We laughed and yes, we even cried. I bought fun matching pajamas for all of us and took plenty of silly pictures in our matchy-matchy PJ's! I'm thankful for these memories and I'll forever be grateful God gave us this time together. Yet, this didn't remove the missing and the sadness, knowing that she would not be here with us to celebrate another holiday. It hangs there like a heavy weight upon my back. But, ready or not, here it comes.

There is no stopping time and for the sake of the rest of my family members I was left trying to figure out how best to balance all of this. My little boy deserves a fun, happy Christmas and it is exactly what Melanie would want for him. I'm positive of this. She loved the holidays, and she wouldn't want me to be overwhelmed with sadness. So, what did I do? I went to the place where I know I can go, day or night, and laid my heart on the altar.

During the early morning as I lifted this care up to my Heavenly Father, He reminded me of the parable in Matthew 6:26 – 34 about the birds of the field. My paraphrase, *"if God cares about the birds and the flowers and grass, does he not care more about us?"* The last verse is what really got me, *"Give your entire attention to what God is doing right now, and don't get worked up about what may or may not happen tomorrow. God will help you deal with whatever hard things come up when the time comes"* Matthew 6:34 MSG.

So, I decided for that first Christmas without Melanie I would set a new goal for myself. I was not going to worry about the fact that I didn't buy one gift and I wasn't going to worry about what we will or will not do. I didn't have all the answers, but I was going to do my best to trust in my Heavenly Father who cares so much more for me than the birds of the field. I don't want to fear, and I don't want to worry. I didn't know what the holiday season would look like, but I was certain of one thing – I'm going to place my hope and trust in God who will pave the way for me as He always has.

Moment of Reflection: How can you prepare for the holidays? Did you do something special to remember your loved one during this time?

CHAPTER 35

Pandemic Grief

I've been thinking about how different it is walking through the grief journey in the middle of a pandemic. Walking through grief is tough enough under normal circumstances but trying to manage all of this during a pandemic is on a completely different level. It's been heartbreaking for those who couldn't honor and celebrate the life of their loved one due to the Covid restrictions.

Yes, grief is like the waves in the ocean. It absolutely ebbs and flows and we never know when another wave is going to hit us and take us under. I live for the days when my grief is calm and less like a hurricane.

Grief is also like a long hike through the wilderness, too. The path has many twists and turns and is often laden with rocks, some so big that I have a hard time maneuvering around them. Then, there are other paths that are scattered with small stones which are much more manageable.

During this time one of the hardest things was figuring out how to best manage through the waves and the wilderness without the direct support of those in my tribe and those who I love most. I so missed my dearest friends and family who don't live near me.

This was a time when we most needed to be together – hugging, holding, sharing, or simply, just being together, yet due to the pandemic this was prohibited.

Hurdling the boulders of grief has been the hardest, most challenging thing I've ever encountered. Each of these boulders have names and some I know better than others: Sadness, Anger, Anxiety, Disbelief, Lethargy, Foggy Brain, and Numbness, just to name a few. Some of these big boulders are behind me, but I'm not foolish enough to think I may never encounter them again. I'm sure as I continue moving forward, I will likely go around a corner and there will be yet another one staring me in the face.

While there are so many unknowns in this world, I cling to the things I am certain of. I know there is hope during loss. I know that we can grieve with hope. It doesn't mean I won't be sad sometimes, and it doesn't mean I won't cry because I surely will. My hope and my trust rest in Jesus. There is no other I can run to in the dark of the night with my questions, worries and fears. He's the one I turn to in the early mornings as I'm looking at the picture of my beautiful girl, next to an urn of ashes. His word is true, and he is my promise-keeper.

Moment of Reflection – What do you know for certain in your life? Where do you turn for help?

CHAPTER 36

He Knows

God knows that I have already spent years mourning the death of my girl. This was long before she went to heaven. The daughter I knew and loved slowly disappeared in front of my eyes as the drugs overtook her mind and body. After I learned that addiction was a disease, I was able to view things through a different lens, but it still didn't take the sadness away. The same is true today.

God knows I'm still wrestling within. He knows that I always will. Yes, I know she's safe and I know she's at peace. I know she is no longer struggling, but still, my momma's heart wrestles with her simply being gone from this earth. But He knows.

I refuse to allow the moment of Melanie's death to steal all the beautiful memories I have of her life. I know it's easy to focus on the death of our loved ones. After all, we miss everything about them: their voice, laughter, touch, smile and most of all, their unique presence in our lives. Each person fills a unique role and it's a place no one else can fill. We will never stop missing them, but for me it's important that I continue to live. I'm not saying it's easy, but our time here on this earth is not done. I want to honor my daughter in a positive way and am trusting God to show me what that looks like. I have other family members who love and need me. Just as we miss our loved one, our family probably misses us, too. Let's face it, this grief journey has stolen moments, hours, days, months and for some even years of the lives we have.

I've made a commitment to myself that I will take each day and live it the best I can. I know Melanie would not want me living a life steeped in overwhelming grief and heaviness. I believe we can be both grieving and blessed at the same time. One doesn't cancel out the other. It doesn't mean I won't have moments of sadness, and it doesn't mean I won't miss her. My love for her will never end, and I'll miss her every single day of my life until we meet again in heaven. But I'm choosing to live for her each day and instead of focusing on her death, I will focus on her life.

He truly does know the pain we suffer due to our losses and our grief. Especially on the days when the waves of loss try to take me under, I am determined to run to Jesus. I will seek his face and his heart of love and compassion.

He knows the days without our loved ones can be circuitous. But even during all the ups and downs I see God making a new path. *"Be alert, be present. I'm about to do something brand-new. It's bursting out! Don't you see it? There it is! I'm making a road through the desert, rivers through the badlands"* (Isaiah 43:19).

I don't know what this new path will entail. But I do believe God will turn this devastating loss into something good. Somehow, he will make a way where there doesn't seem to be one. If anyone can do this he can. Melanie's life will not be in vain and I will share her story to bring life and hope to others.

Moment of Reflection – If we remove expectations would that help us find peace when we don't have all the answers?

CHAPTER 37

King of My Heart

For some reason there is something about the changing of the season that causes me to become more reflective as many thoughts and memories have been flooding my mind. Both the good and the challenging. I'm sure some of you may be thinking, "Challenging! Girl, I've gone through some downright horrible, terrible, bad things in my life." Yes, I'm sure you have. I have too, but bear with me for a moment.

When I looked up the definition of the word challenge, specifically, "What is the meaning of challenges in life?" it says: *challenge noun (DIFFICULT JOB) – (the situation of being faced with) something that needs great mental or physical effort in order to be done successfully and therefore tests a person's ability*

When Melanie went on to Heaven, I couldn't think of anything worse that could have happened in my life or to our family. There was no doubt that I would need the greatest amount of physical and mental effort ever required of me if I was going to survive this. To say that walking this grief journey is something that tests my ability is an understatement. On some days my ability to simply put one foot in front of the other is more than I can manage. However, I decided early on that I would not allow the enemy to steal anything further from me and I would meet this challenge head-on. The only way I knew how to fight this battle was spiritually:

"God is strong, and he wants you strong. So, take everything the Master has set out for you, well-made weapons of the best materials. And put them to use so you will be able to stand up to everything the Devil throws your way. This is no weekend war that we'll walk away from and forget about in a couple of hours. This is for keeps, a life-or-death fight to the finish against the Devil and all his angels.

Be prepared. You're up against far more than you can handle on your own. Take all the help you can get, every weapon God has issued, so that when it's all over but the shouting you'll still be on your feet. Truth, righteousness, peace, faith, and salvation are more than words. Learn how to apply them. You'll need them throughout your life. God's Word is an indispensable weapon. In the same way, prayer is essential in this ongoing warfare. Pray hard and long. Pray for your brothers and sisters. Keep your eyes open. Keep each other's spirits up so that no one falls behind or drops out." (Ephesians 6:12 – 18 MSG)

Just like many of you, I'm walking this grief journey day by day. It's taken my breath away and left me moving like one of the zombies from The Walking Dead. There have been days when I've been curled up in a ball staring out the window, and other days when I'm walking like a warrior. I begin to realize, all the ups and downs, twists and turns are all part of this journey called Grief.

Then deep within my spirit I am reminded that God is a God of light, love, and life! Our Heavenly Father is life, and He has already taken the keys of death from the enemy. On those days when the challenges try to take over my heart and mind, I turn to the only one who can lift me like no other – The King of My Heart. My faith and trust in God are all that I have left, and I know in my heart that God can and will turn this around – somehow, someday for His good.

Moment of Reflection – Who do you run to when your heart is deeply hurting?

CHAPTER 38

The Anchor

I have close friends who are avid sailors. They love going out on the water, feeling the rush of the wind through the sails and the warmth of the sun on their faces. Sometimes they take friends with them on these trips. As close as we are, I inwardly pray they never ask us to be their guests.

I'm not the best swimmer and the thought of being out on the open sea terrifies me. Even though I will likely never be in that position I found myself thinking about the "what ifs". What would I do if we found ourselves on a boat in the middle of the ocean? What if a storm came? What if we couldn't find land? What if we kept drifting further out into deeper waters never to found again?

Then I started thinking about the anchor. Could it help me?

Every anchor I've seen is a huge, heavy, sturdy, unbreakable piece of iron attached to a long, long rope or chain. When my friends settle in for the night, I imagine they throw that heavy anchor overboard confidently knowing it will do what it's supposed to do, which is keeping them in one general area instead of drifting out to sea while they are sleeping.

As my mind continued to wander, I began to think about the rope the anchor is tied to. What if the rope broke away from the anchor? What would happen then? As heavy as the anchor may be what good will it do if the rope is not strong and sturdy? If the rope breaks then the anchor, even though it's made from a heavy piece of iron, would sink, and be entrenched in the bottom of the ocean and we would be left adrift.

The more I contemplated this I realized it is not only important to have a heavy anchor, but you need to be certain the anchor is attached to an equally strong piece of rope that can withstand the rough seas. Suddenly this became a lightbulb moment for me.

How much is the anchor and the rope just like us and our relationship with Jesus?

For me, during this grief journey I've said repeatedly that Jesus is my anchor. He's the one thing that has kept me afloat during the stormy days of grief. Jesus promised to send us his Spirit to be our Helper and our Comforter *(John 14:14 – 31)*. So, if Jesus is our anchor, then the Holy Spirit is our rope. We cannot have one without the other.

During times of overwhelming darkness, when you are so tired from fighting the heaviness of grief, your anchor should strengthen you, but you should also be encouraged by the rope.

While I may never physically be out on the ocean waters, it's become clearer to me that if I cling to my anchor, Jesus, then I will also be tethered to the Holy Spirit – the strongest rope we could ever dream of having and one that will never fray or break.

Moment of Reflection: How strong is the rope that is connected to your anchor?

CHAPTER 39

Let the Truth Be Told

D o you remember the old kids rhyme, "Liar, liar, pants on fire?" Oh, I'm sure we've all said that in our little 5-year-old sing-songy voice to one friend or another at some point in our lives. Even now when I think about the word liar it's cringeworthy. I've always considered myself to be a truth teller and have raised our children to be honest and have integrity. Did I always tell the truth? Was I always honest when asked a question? I thought when I finally removed my mask I no longer had to fake it and began living a more authentic life. Now here I am wondering if that's really true.

Now before I get totally carried away and send out the condemnation police, I'm going to cut myself a little slack here. I don't know how you were raised, but I was told, *"Never air your dirty laundry in public."* Does that sound familiar to you? Or how about, *"Always keep a stiff upper lip."* I was raised not to tell anyone outside of our home about any problems we may be having. Anytime someone asked how I was I quickly responded, "I'm doing *GREEAAT!*" Oh, I'm sure I probably sounded a little like Tony the Tiger, but at least I didn't let on that anything bad was happening in my life! I'm sure we all know people like this today. I know someone who would rather walk on hot coals than let you know there was anything but total peace and harmony in her household.

When someone you love dies it's kind of hard to fake a smile, and if you've been raised like I was it's equally as difficult to just let your emotions flow naturally. One of the things I've learned during this grief journey is to be honest, both with myself and those who are in my life.

I've had encounters with some who clearly wished I'd simply said I was fine when asked how I was doing. It was very clear that my honest answer made them uncomfortable.

Providing a false answer may make it easy on others, but it's like a stab to the heart for us. Being able to walk in our truth is what's healthier for us. After all, we are the ones walking this winding road called grief where among the quiet streams, could be a pitfall just around the corner.

No matter where you are on this grief journey – whether it's days, months or even years, this road is hard and it hurts. There are moments when the tears come out of nowhere. Guess what? It's OK to *not* be OK! Tears are truly healing and cleansing. So instead of bottling all of that up inside of you, feel the freedom to no longer be strong or stoic. Being sad or shedding tears is not a sign of weakness. It is a sign of strength.

I absolutely love this scripture, *"You keep track of all my sorrows. You have collected all my tears in your bottle. You have recorded each one in your book" (Psalm 56:8 NLT).* And we need to remember, even Jesus wept.

Moment of Reflection: Have you found yourself being cautious with your feelings to protect others? Beginning today give yourself permission to no longer keep that "stiff upper lip" and allow yourself to let the truth be told.

CHAPTER 40

Yearning to Soothe the Savage Beast Within Me

S everal months after Melanie died I had the chance to catch up on the phone with a longtime friend. Interestingly, when the topic turned to Melanie and I expressed my sadness over missing my girl she said, "Really? You're *still* feeling this way?" Wow! It was the first time anyone had spoken those words out loud to me. By the tone in her voice, I could sense she was sincere in asking this question. Society often places a time limit on a person's grief, and it is so unrealistic.

This gave me the opportunity to share that there will be no amount of time that will ever go by when I will not grieve the loss of my child. Melanie is a part of me. Flesh of my flesh and bone of my bone. I will forever miss her and grieve the fact that she is not here to share our lives together.

I was also able to share that thankfully, I now have sad moments in a day, instead of full days or weeks of sadness.

Yes, the savage beast of grief still rears its ugly head and hits me from out of nowhere, but I continue to walk through it, hand in hand with God leading the way. It's my faith that sustains me every single day.

When you suffer a loss of any kind, I think it's important that you allow yourself to feel it. Experience it. And equally as important you should find those things which help lift you up. These are a few things that helped me walk through this grief journey:

Grief counseling – I didn't do this right away. I was never one who was fond of therapy, but in this instance, I have found it to be quite helpful. I encourage you to find someone who is a good fit for you, and where you can speak with them on a regular basis.

Music – I'm sure you've heard the old saying *music soothes the savage beast*. Well, it really does, and grief is a beast like no other! I listen to music throughout each day that uplifts me. Oftentimes it's Christian music, but there are also times I want to hear some of the old songs that take me back to an earlier, carefree time. Where you may feel heaviness, music, and the words within make your heart feel lighter. Give it a try.

Me-Time – Now this can mean different things to different people, but when I'm overwhelmed or feeling stressed, I need a little "me-time." I may just need to go for a short walk by myself. Other times, I go to another part of the house and read quietly for a while. I like to treat myself to a massage or a facial. When Melanie died a dear friend bought me two beautiful candles with Melanie's picture on it. These personalized candles were so very special. Each day when I get up in the early morning hours to spend my quiet time with the Lord, I light them. The ones my friend bought me have long since burned out, but I have continued to buy candles with my girl's picture on it. My favorite scent is Autumn Leaves and I select different pictures of Melanie to put on each candle.

Moment of Reflection - What gives your heart, mind and body peace and relief? What is the emotional value of me-time?

CHAPTER 41

Who's Your Daddy?

*R*emember the Titans is one of my all-time favorite movies for so many reasons. It's based on the true story of African American coach Herman Boone, played by Denzel Washington, and his attempt to integrate a high school football team in 1970's Alexandria, VA.

There is one line in the movie where Coach Boone asks one of the main characters, "Who's Your Daddy?" The line crossed my mind recently when my son received an assignment in his discipleship class to list 20 names to describe Jesus. He came up with about 8 of them quickly but the first one was, Father.

After the first year of grieving Melanie, it touched my heart deeply that this was the first name he thought of. It wasn't that long ago when he asked me, "Why didn't God intervene and stop Melanie from dying?" It's a very valid question, isn't it? If you've lost a loved one and are on this grief journey I'm certain you and your family have asked the same question, haven't you?

Losing someone changes you. You will never be the same person you once were.

The death of a loved one changes you. It challenges everything about us that used to be right or normal. Physically we may no longer feel well. Anxiety, fear, and actual pain afflict our bodies when we may have otherwise been strong and healthy.

Emotionally we are challenged at every turn. The tears seem to flow at the drop of a hat. We thought we were strong and now we may look at it as a weakness.

Many who had a strong relationship with God now question, lash out and even turn away from him. That's ok. He has big shoulders and can handle it. He understands. After all, he had to watch his own son be executed and die a slow, painful death.

All of these things are perfectly normal now. Losing my daughter has changed me in more ways than I would have ever imagined. And you know what? I will not apologize for it. A piece of me and my heart is missing, and until the day I see her again I will never be the same.

Give yourself the grace you need to get through each day. I believe our hearts will slowly heal in a way that allows us to live each moment, but the scars from our loss will forever remain deep within us. We will never be the same person as we once were.

One of the most common questions we ask when a loved one dies is, Why? It may only be 3 letters, but they hold a powerful punch. When I first learned of Melanie's death I certainly asked God that question. I think we would almost be unhuman if we didn't wonder why. However, we can make a choice and hold on to the why, or we can put our faith and trust in God.

I am thankful that I had a firm foundation in my faith when Melanie went on to heaven. While it didn't eliminate me from asking the question why, it helped sustain me during this tumultuous journey.

Sometimes in life we'll never receive an answer to the question of *Why* on this side of heaven. But, if you know who your Daddy is, rest assured He will remain right by your side during the highs, and especially during the lows. When we ask why it doesn't make you a bad Christian, it makes you a kid asking your Daddy a valid question.

> **Moment of Reflection** – What are the characteristics of a good father that resonate in your heart? Do you look to Jesus for them?

CHAPTER 42

Trusting When You Can't See

S ince Melanie went on to heaven, I discovered that my stress level increased exponentially and my tolerance for things became quite low. The things I used to take in stride have now become like mountains instead of molehills.

Any discussion surrounding death or illness became a trigger for me, taking me back to *that* day - reliving every horrific word and moment in the days following her death. Pictures which have formed in my mind that cannot be erased. Walking this grief journey is no joke and as much as I wish it weren't true, no amount of time will ever make it completely disappear.

From the moment I heard the words "your daughter is dead," I knew there would only be one way I would survive child loss. I placed my broken heart and totally crushed spirit in the hands of my Heavenly Father knowing it would be the only way I could do it. It's still the toughest thing I'll ever have to walk through, but I can't imagine being alone in my grief.

If you're reading this and struggling, know that you don't have to do this alone. On those days when you feel as if you can barely walk, we can limp along together. And on those days when you feel strong, we can link arms, stand tall and help others who are on the same road. No matter where you are on this journey, you don't have to do this alone.

No, the memories won't ever go away, but the other thing that will never go away - my faith in God. Even during those first dark, devastating hours the one thing I felt more than the overwhelming sadness and disbelief that my girl was gone from this earth, was the holy presence of my Heavenly Father. I felt his arms embrace me in a way I had never, ever felt before. They lifted me up and held me close. It made me realize that God isn't just in the high places, like Heaven. He is in the low, dark places. He is on the ground with us. Weeping. Hugging. Holding and lifting us up in his arms. I could never have made it this far without him and without my faith in him. I still don't have any answers to the "Why now, God?" but I trust him with my whole heart even when I can't see him.

Trust in the Lord completely, and do not rely on your own opinions. With all your heart rely on him to guide you, and he will lead you in every decision you make. Become intimate with him in whatever you do, and he will lead you wherever you go. (Proverbs 3:5-6 TPT).

He continues to be my Comforter, Encourager, and Healer.

Moment of Reflection: Who do you place your heart, trust, and soul in when you have no answers?

CHAPTER 43

The Gifts of Grief: Friendship and New Understanding

We can look at the grief chart and have an intellectual knowledge and understanding that we are going to go through each step of the grief cycle. But on an emotional level, it's so very different. In my mind I thought, I'll just have to go through these 6 cycles and then, I'll be ok. Oh, how wrong I was! One of the things I have found so frustrating is that we can end up going through some of the steps repeatedly. You think you're doing so well and then, Wham! Out of nowhere you're back underwater again.

One day I was speaking with a friend who was also experiencing loss and we were sharing how the stress of grief has been affecting us physically. I had been feeling so terribly empty and drained. It's so unbelievable how the body literally breaks down under the weight of grief and the stress that accompanies it. We know it's so important for us to care for ourselves during this time, but it's one of the last things we often do.

As we recalled some of the really difficult challenges we each faced as young, single moms my friend reminded me of how strong we truly are. She not only reminded me of some of the things we had been through, but more importantly how God was the one who brought us through it all.

143

We've done life together. We've been there for one another through life's ups and downs. No matter where we are, no matter what's happening in our lives we can lift one another up to our Heavenly Father who is always with us. It's our faith that keeps us going day after dark day until the sun begins to shine once again.

At first glance, I would imagine you would never consider grief being a gift, would you? But just think about it for a brief moment. Do you look at people differently now? Do you offer more compassion? Less judgment? More grace? Have your priorities changed? I know mine have. Although work is important and a means to live and pay bills, my mindset has shifted. Spending time with my family has always been a strong priority for me, but since my daughter ran ahead to heaven, my family is my absolute #1 priority!

Once you've suffered the loss of a loved one, especially an unexpected or out of order death, you hold on just a bit tighter to those around you. You appreciate those who surround you, who are there for you and lift you up.

You don't hold on to the small stuff any longer. In fact, you may also realize some of the things you once considered to be extremely important, now looking at it through the new lens of grief, is really small stuff after all. We shrug that off our shoulders now. We have a keen sense of what is truly important, and do you know what? It's no longer things, it's people!

Although I wish I never found myself on this journey, if you ask me if grief has given me a gift, I'd have to say yes, it has. It's given me the gift of a new and clearer perspective, with eyes and a heart to see who and what is most important in my life. God, Family, True Friends. Grief takes so much from us, but it also gives. We learn to love more deeply and hug those closest to us more tightly. We show up more fiercely and we forgive swiftly. Grief heightens the fragility and briefness of life and while it hurts like hell it's a gift received.

Moment of Reflection: What gifts have you received while walking through the grief journey?

CHAPTER 44

Dry Bones Rattle

As each month passed by since Melanie's death, I found myself taking three steps forward then two steps back. It's a dance I play with myself. Oh, there are days I'm feeling strong and healthy. Then there are those days when I feel nothing. Broken and empty, like dry bones rattling. Have you ever felt that way, too?

I know the grief journey ebbs and flows, and for that I'm grateful. Walking in the valley all the time is exhausting. But don't mistake those times I am able to walk in joy with the assumption I no longer miss my girl. My grief will be a part of me for as long as my love for her exists - and that will be forever. I will always miss my child. Don't ever ask me if I'm over it, not even a little.

Nothing about this grief journey is easily navigated. Nothing about this walk is easy. One moment I'm seemingly fine, and strong. Encouraging. Reassuring. Inspiring others. Hopeful. Pouring out my heart for all the world to see, yet I still feel sad, and grief-stricken. The enemy tries to tell me I'm a fraud. A hypocrite. "How can you feel hopeful during loss?" he whispers. "How can you encourage others when you're still grieving?" he taunts. "Melanie is still dead. You're still here. Your own family is still suffering the loss of your girl."

I'm sure we would all agree that grief is hard. It's surely the toughest road I've ever had to walk. Yet as I begin to look at it in a slightly different way, I understand why it's so stinking hard.

I once read where there is much grief, there is much love. I believe this to be true. So, grief is just love with no place to go. As we remember that, maybe it will help us smile through the tears.

On those days I'm not strong, it feels as if grief has sucked all life from these bones and all happiness from my heart. I've never claimed to be a Superhero but I do have one Superpower to extinguish the fiery darts of the enemy. Prayer and the mighty, powerful name of Jesus. When I begin to get beat down, and believe the lies being thrown at me, that's when I run back into my Daddy's arms. I fall on my knees seeking out the only one who can ease the ache of these dry bones and help restore my soul.

In Ezekiel 4:6-7, the Lord shows Ezekiel a valley of dry, dead, brittle bones. *"Then he told me to speak to the bones and say: "O dry bones, listen to the words of God, for the Lord God says, 'See! I am going to make you live and breathe again! I will replace the flesh and muscles on you and cover you with skin. I will put breath into you, and you shall live and know I am the Lord.'"*

Yes, even though these dry bones are rattling, I will stand and praise Jesus for the life I've been given. I may not understand it all, but one day when I see him face to face, I'll know. When I see my girl, these dry bones will dance again.

Moment of Reflection: Have you experienced the brittle feeling of dryness in your bones? What do you do when you feel ready to break?

CHAPTER 45

Can We Have A Retake?

My son's school set a date to retake school pictures. It got me thinking about do overs, second chances and retakes. How amazing would it be if we could manage all of life's challenges by asking for a retake?

Recently a friend asked if I relived the day Melanie went to heaven. Did I think about it over and over again? This question opened the door for a deep-hearted conversation about those last hours before I was certain she was gone from this world. But more importantly, we talked about what I had learned that day and how it continued to impact my heart and mind.

As much as I wish it were possible, you can't unhear or unsee things, no matter how much time passes. After reading police and autopsy reports, which were graphic enough for any James Patterson novel, I have formed a picture in my mind of my girl's last moments. It's not of the beautiful girl I knew and loved. What enters our mind, eyes and heart then creates images which oftentimes haunts us.

Soon I began to wonder why it's taken me this long to realize that I don't have to allow the enemy to torture my mind and heart this way. I don't have to relive *those* memories! I have other pictures and memories to draw from that are so much more beautiful!

We all grieve differently, and we all heal differently. We don't look the same or act the same. So why would anyone think we should heal the same? Healing unfolds in its own time. Don't allow others to place you in a box and dictate when you should be "over it." I encourage you to seek support and encouragement along this most difficult journey. Don't allow others to dictate how you should feel. We will always miss our children, our husbands, our siblings, our parents. Always! I believe God continues to heal our broken hearts, but the reality of it is your healing will likely come in stages. In your own time. Be kind and gentle with yourself.

One day we will be able to remember how blessed we were to have known their love, with joy and not heartache or grief.

As a Believer we can bring our heartfelt prayers and requests to the feet of our Heavenly Father. Prayer is our greatest weapon, and we can come to him and ask for a retake by saying:

"Father, in Jesus' name I thank you that we can come to you anywhere and at any time. You are our greatest weapon, Lord. You hear our heart's cry, and we know that nothing is impossible with you. I am asking you to renew my mind and heart. Thank you for giving me the retake I need to live this life peacefully. Instead of dwelling on the last moments of my child's life I thank you for giving me a retake, a new picture. One that depicts the beautiful young woman Melanie was in you. Thank you that the picture I will now hold near to my heart is of beauty and the happy moments she lived, not died. No matter how I may feel, your word and promises are true. You are doing a new thing. You are creating a path through the wilderness and streams through the desert. Thank you for loving me and healing my heart and mind, in Jesus name."

Moment of Reflection: Are you looking for a retake?

CHAPTER 46

Speak Words of Life Over Your Fragile Heart

I sn't it amazing how one of the smallest parts of our body is both the strongest and the deadliest? Some may think it's the heart, or perhaps the lungs. Those certainly are major parts of our body that give us life and strength, but it is not the part I am referring to. A small yet strong part is, the tongue. *"The tongue has the power of life and death" (Proverbs 18:21 NIV).*

The power of the tongue and the words we say don't just impact others. The words we speak about ourselves can have life altering repercussions. Perhaps you've heard the scripture from Matthew 12:34, *"out of the abundance of the heart the mouth speaks."* What you think and ultimately say about yourself can breathe life or death into existence.

Our tongue and the words that so easily roll off it can either help build others up, or they can tear them down. Just a few simple words can destroy a life, a friendship, a family.

How many times when you've been feeling down have you said things like, *I'm so depressed. I'm so sick. I hate this life. I don't want to live like this anymore. I give up?* These are words of death you're speaking over yourself! The next time you're feeling down, raise your head a little higher and look up! Even if you don't feel it, speak out loud and speak kind, loving words to yourself.

No matter how long you've been walking along the road of grief and heartache - 1 day, 1 week, 1 month or multiple years, we should not be expected to hold it all together all the time. There will be moments I refer to as grief bursts. It's ok to have these moments. Cry, scream, shout, rest, walk, run like the wind. But never, ever give up! Don't talk badly about yourself either. Be gentle with your own heart. There is hope during loss! But it all begins and ends with who you're running to for your strength. Get refilled by the only one who never tires, never leaves, and will always be with you along the way. His name is Jesus.

Before grief became a part of my life I was a perfectionist. It was my way of keeping control and order in my life - something I needed since there were other areas I had no control over. When death came crashing through my door it became harder to maintain and it's actually been a bit of a relief to let some of that go. I no longer need to have every single thing in my life perfect. I love how God is using my brokenness to perfect within me the things he wants to change and control. It's in my brokenness I've found an even greater thing - an ability to totally surrender to him. This is where his light comes in and shines the brightest. We are all broken – but that's how the light gets in.

Moment of Reflection: Spend a few moments writing down some life-giving phrases you can hold onto.

CHAPTER 47

The Battle to Be Authentic

As I've said, when Melanie first went to heaven I stepped out in faith and removed the mask I'd been wearing for many years. It was a giant step for me, but it was one full of fear. Fear of being judged. Fear of being shunned. Fear of tarnishing her memory. Fear of just about everything. At the time it felt good to let down my guard and remove my mask. Freeing. It was heavier than I had ever realized.

There were periods of time that old familiar feeling began to creep back in, and I would find myself stumbling around on this journey. The waves would begin crashing down all around me and I'd come up gasping for air feeling overwhelmed, again. Should I be doing better than I am? Did I already go through that step in the grief process? How am I back here again? I had someone tell me at 7 months into my grief journey "it was time for me to pull myself up by my bootstraps and move on." This well-intentioned person had never experienced child loss and had no clue what they were talking about. So, I enlightened them.

Those who have never walked this journey are usually the ones who impart their "wisdom" and tell us how we should feel. Though they may mean well, it places unrealistic expectations upon us. We then feel as if we're not measuring up. We end up feeling like we should be at a certain place, and feel a certain way, within a certain timeframe. What those well-meaning people don't realize is, each person's grief journey is their own. There is no set timeframe.

Unfortunately, as a result of these types of comments, I began to wear my mask again and the weight of it began to take its toll on me, both physically and emotionally. As my physical body deteriorated, it invited my old friend, Fear, in. Fear causes stress and stress produces anxiety. It's like being on the worst merry-go-round ride ever!

When someone would ask, "How are you?" my immediate answer would be, "Fine." Even if underneath I was actually feeling broken, sad, scared, confused, fragile, or crushed.

Can you relate? Why do we do it? Is it to save the other person or ourselves?

At first I thought it was a good idea to answer so honestly but as time went on I realized most people didn't really want to hear the truth, so the word, Fine, became my standard answer to cover us both.

Thankfully, as I've continued down this path, which continues to ebb and flow, I now know who I can bare my heart to. It's not everyone, but a few in my intimate circle of friends. We don't have to feel guilty about what may seem like a lie either. We don't have to get naked in front of all to see, which is similar to what we are doing when we are sharing our broken hearts and feelings. So, I've come to like the word fine now. It protects me in a way I never realized before.

Someone I respect, who has helped me walk this path, gave me an excellent piece of advice which helped free me, once again. She said, "Pat, you need to stop being strong and take that mask off! Stop trying to handle it all and stop swallowing all your tears and sadness. Let them flow. Be who you are in this season of your grief journey. It's okay to let people see your tears."

I've often said, tears are cleansing, and I truly believe that. However, there has also been that little voice inside my head that says, "You're a cry baby! Get over it – people die! And the loudest voice I heard was, "No one wants to hear you crying about Melanie anymore. You're going to lose all of your friends and family if you keep this up!"

So, when I was told I should remove my mask and be who I am in that moment of time, I swallowed hard and cried. Tears that I'd been keeping pent up flowed. Tears for the loss of my girl who I love and miss terribly. Tears for all that will never be.

There were also tears of gratitude to God for giving me my girl for 38 years. For some parents that is a lifetime longer than what they had.

A child's death changes a person forever. Grief is lifelong. It doesn't just go away or disappear after a certain period of time passes by. Mercifully, it softens but it's always there, tucked away in a corner of your heart.

One important thing to try and remember is this - You are not alone. There are others to help lift us up along the road, but placing our faith in God, knowing He walks by our side every moment of every day guarantees we will not have to do this by ourselves. *God carries us through the storm – Is 43:2*

Each day my goal is to remember that God is always with me, walking beside me and lifting my head. *"But You, LORD, are a shield around me, my glory, and the One who lifts my head"* (Psalm 3:3 NASB)

Moment of Reflection: Do you feel the need to put on a strong face/mask when you actually feel weak? Are you afraid to be who you truly are?

CHAPTER 48

My A-Ha Moment

As is typical of most women, and especially mothers, we are always running around taking care of everyone else. We have many roles and juggle so many things we could easily work for Barnum & Bailey! Cook. Taxi driver. Social director. Wife. Mother. Lover. Friend. Teacher. Nurse. Cleaning Lady. The list goes on and on, and in many cases, this is all on top of holding down a full-time job. With responsibilities like this, it's not surprising that taking care of ourselves falls to the bottom, the way, way bottom, of the list.

As I muddled through the first year of loss, I learned how deeply grief can affect your life. I realized I didn't have the physical, mental, or emotional capacity to do all the things I could before. I began reprioritizing my life so I could concentrate on my own self-care.

I had a full-time job and a family to take care of, along with trying to keep up with my personal blog where I share my heart while walking this grief journey. I began to hit a wall and realized I needed to scale back – my physical, spiritual, and emotional well-being desperately needed attention. The heaviness and weight of losing a loved one creates stress and anxiety that often lead to actual physical illness. It is debilitating and if left untreated can often lead to serious health consequences.

It's so important to take care of ourselves while we are walking this grief journey as we cannot be there for our other family members and loved ones if we don't take care of ourselves. Just like the flight attendant says, "Put the oxygen mask on yourself first before putting it on anyone else."

After a period of time I began to see some light at the end of what had been several weeks of darkness. During this time of self-care I had a few A-Ha moments I'd like to share.

My 1st A-Ha moment: It's OK if you aren't strong, and it's OK to cry!

Really, it is! No more swallowing tears and no more Wonder Woman routines! I read a fabulous article based on the Bible's shortest scripture, *Jesus wept*. It touched my heart because it shows the utter humanness of Jesus. Even though he knew the final outcome, he still had a grieving heart. Jesus already knew the will of God and he certainly was aware that Lazarus would be returned to life. He didn't weep because of any uncertainty in his ability to do this miracle. Jesus wept because he was a human being, a man, who had feelings like you and me and he understood the grief of those around him.

Even though Jesus knew Lazarus would rise and live he cried because he was grieving for his friends. He mourned. He knew what it meant to be heartbroken and crushed in spirit. If crying is good enough for Jesus, it's good enough for me!

My 2nd A-Ha moment: I'm no longer going to worry about whether my crying, sadness and grief makes others uncomfortable.

If you have not experienced child loss, I understand why you have no idea why I'm still sad, crying or grieving and you know what? I am so happy you have no idea why I feel this way. Tears and sadness are all a part of the grief journey. There is no time limit either. Tears are just another form of all the love we have stored up in heart for our loved one. Grief IS love!

My 3rd A-Ha moment: It's OK to take time for YOU!

Since your loved one died, has your physical and mental well-being suffered? I know it has for me. I have been ignoring my own well-being since Melanie went to heaven and if I'm totally honest, I've probably been ignoring my health for years leading up to her death.

When you have a loved one who suffers from a disease, you become a caretaker. You are so busy taking care of the one who is ill, you ignore your own health and well-being. If I want to be here for my youngest son and family it's time for some changes. Instead of putting ourselves last on the list, we must intentionally focus on ourselves. Of course, this means different things to each of us.

I have found that during this point in my life starting small is what works best for me. These are just a few things I started doing to begin taking back my physical and emotional health:

- Walk each day for 30 minutes. I remind myself, my pace may be slow but I'm not in a race.
- Drink 64 oz. of water.
- Take a few minutes each day to pray or meditate. I never meditated before and I wasn't sure how good I'd be at it, but I downloaded the Calm app and it helped teach me how to breathe deeply. It is rather amazing what slowing down and taking some deep breaths can do for you! I also use this app when I can't sleep at night. It has some nice relaxing music.
- Crocheting is something that is peaceful and calming for me. Perhaps for you it's knitting, painting or cross-stitch, but doing something with our hands, is therapeutic. I can sit and crochet while listening to music, a podcast or simply nothing at all.

I'm no expert, but I am a woman and a mother walking this rocky road of grief and I have come to see how important it is for us to use self-care. It is not an act of selfishness but is healthy and good for me. It's an act of trying to preserve what is left of us as we walk along the valley of the shadow of death.

My faith is what continues to sustain me and the time I spend throughout the day with my Heavenly Father is what gives me the strength to face each day. I continue to take each day, one step and one breath at a time.

Moment of Reflection: What have your A-Ha moments revealed to you? What sustains you during the dark moments of this journey?

CHAPTER 49

Life is a Journey – Not a Race

As I've been writing this book there was no way around the fact that I had to dig deep down into the well of memories of my life with Melanie. Every time I reeled the bucket back up to the surface, it was chock full of both good and bad images. How we got to this point has been painful, and many times, very sad.

Substance Use Disorder (SUD) is a very misunderstood disease. With each chapter written I have found myself, in my mind, walking down small, intersecting alleyways much like you find on the streets of Venice. You never know when or if one will intersect with the other. Some of the alleyways can be very dark and other times, as you're walking the tiny cobblestone streets, out of nowhere you find yourself looking up into the most beautiful, bright, colorful piazza! The sight is just magnificent!

Writing this book about our life reminds me of those alleyways – the dark and winding parts that lead up to the day Melanie died, and the beauty of her life intertwined within. When you have a loved one whose life has been taken over by SUD, there are many, many dark moments. Because of that sometimes it's hard to remember the good, but thankfully, this was only a fragment of who Melanie was. Melanie was so much more than the girl who suffered with that disease. She had a heart and spirit made by Jesus and that is the girl I will remember.

So, while having to think and write about the tough times, I also found myself thinking about the moments Melanie left me smiling and laughing. Like one time when she was about 7 years old the two of us went out to breakfast, along with my boyfriend. Before breakfast was even served Melanie was playing around at the table and tipped over a very large glass of orange juice. With those beautiful brown eyes now looking like a deer in the headlights, she quickly hopped up and ran to the restroom to wash her hands, leaving me to quickly clean up her mess. When she returned to the table, she very innocently asked "Mommy, what are those flusher things on the wall in the bathroom?" The look on my boyfriend's face was priceless as we realized she went into the men's room instead of the ladies room! Oh my! All these years later I can laugh out loud at that memory because that was typical Melanie. She was a little bit of innocent and mischief all rolled into one.

Friends, our lives truly are a journey. It's filled with hills and valleys. This is a true statement for everyone, not just those who find themselves on this grief journey. We've often heard the saying, *"It's a marathon, not a sprint."* Life may not be an actual race, but I've found this saying to be true while walking the road of grief. It's okay for us to take time out as we consider how best to manage our new normal. Figuring out our lives without our loved one takes time, and not just days, weeks or even months. Following are some guidelines for those who are training for a marathon, and could easily apply to those of us who are grieving as well:

- **Marathons are hard – really hard!** Well, losing a loved one is hard – really hard!

- **You're never really done.** We will never, ever forget our loved one, so there is always a part of our grief that will remain forever. We just learn to live with it.
- **It's all in the training plan.** I will admit, I'm still working on this. I don't understand the reason for this pain and why my daughter had to die at the young age of 38, but I wholeheartedly trust God's plan for my life, and hers. *"Trust in the Lord with all your heart, lean not to your own understanding but in all your ways acknowledge him and he will direct your path (Proverbs 3:5-6 NIV).*
- **Roadblocks are inevitable.** You may think you've gone through all the stages of grief and all is well, only to discover you may find yourself back at stage 1, or 3, or 2. It's okay. It's part of the process as we peel back each layer of the onion, called our heart.
- **Recovery is just as important as the race.** Give yourself the time you need to recover, and grieve for as long as it takes. Everyone grieves differently. Do not allow anyone else to judge you or influence how long you should walk this grief journey. In fact, I don't believe we actually recover from grief, we just learn how to live our lives around the missing piece of our heart.
- **Nothing is ever easy.** A marathon isn't easy, and neither is grief. Truly it's pretty awful at times. We find ourselves having to push through the dark moments and when you do, you realize you are stronger and more resilient than you ever imagined.

Yes, life is a journey and not a race. You will probably never be the same person you were before your loved one passed away.

And let us run with perseverance the race marked out for us, fixing our eyes on Jesus, the pioneer and perfecter of faith. For the joy set before him he endured the cross, scorning its shame, and sat down at the right hand of the throne of God. Consider him who endured such opposition from sinners, so that you will not grow weary and lose heart (Hebrews 12:1-3 NIV).

Moment of Reflection: What big or small changes can you make in your life to be a journey and not a sprint?

CHAPTER 50

Putting Our Broken Pieces Back Together

Have you ever felt like your life was like a jigsaw puzzle? And I'm not talking about that moment when you triumphantly put that last piece into place and feel so accomplished. No, I'm referring to the 1000-piece puzzle you dump out in the middle of your table. You know how you have to begin the task of sorting through the big messy pile of broken pieces, just to try to get one to fit nicely into another? This is how a person feels when they suffer the loss of a loved one. A big, messy pile of brokenness. You may not know who you are anymore. Many times, along with the loss of our person, we lose our own identity. There are days it's hard to remember the person I was before Melanie ran ahead to heaven. Thankfully, God is a gracious, loving, and merciful God. He is the one that formed me in my mother's womb and says that I am fearfully and wonderfully made. Because He made me, He alone knows how to put me back together.

Yet so often as we grieve our loss we can also find ourselves focusing on the past and all that was. When we dare to even begin looking at the road ahead of us, worry overtakes every part of our being.

How many hours in each day have you spent worrying, replaying events in your mind, asking *why* and *what if*? Has it helped?

Has it alleviated the pain? Has it answered the questions, which probably have no answers on this side of heaven? Oh, my friend, I'm with you on this. I've spent countless hours as I've walked this path wringing my hands and hitting the rewind button in my mind on how I coulda, shoulda, woulda done things differently. In the end, this hasn't helped one bit. But the moment I turn all these questions and cares over to God, even if I don't have the answers yet, I have felt a certain unquestionable peace encompass my soul. Give it a try today. One thing is certain, it can't hurt.

I've been spending a lot of my time with my Heavenly Father, journaling, reading the word, walking and just being still. Sometimes pulling back into a quiet place and being still is the best thing to heal one's heart. *Be still and know that I am God (Psalm 46:11 NLT)*

The worrying that keeps you up at night – the "what if's" swirling around in your head, the fear weighing on your heart and mind, give it to God. Just like the puzzle, I have found that I can sometimes be a jumbled mess, but I am confident it will all become beautiful again one day.

Before Melanie died I had my own ideas of grief. I thought it was a sad time following the death of someone you loved. As each day of this grief journey passes I learn more and more about how little I really know. One thing I know for sure - there is no "getting over" it, but there is hope for walking through it. Step by step. Moment by moment. Grief isn't something you complete, but it is something you learn how to live with.

Coping with your loss also doesn't mean you're over it. Coping doesn't equal moving on. Coping doesn't mean you've forgotten. Coping is being able to smile without feeling massive amounts of guilt that you're happy. Coping is feeling like you can breathe again without feeling overwhelmed. Coping is normal and healthy, and it doesn't mean you love any less.

Some days I may find it harder than others to share what's on my heart. For a brief moment I may even wonder what others may think of me, laying it all out there for everyone to see. Then, I think about this - if the sadness, hurt and heartache I'm having to walk through become steppingstones of hope for others then it's all worth it! I pray that other people will find healing in my wounds.

Each day may be different, but as I hold on to my faith I know my broken heart will mend. It will always have the cracks and scars that were formed from the grief, but I'll always remember great love was born from it.

Moment of Reflection: It takes time to put a puzzle together, often it doesn't happen overnight. What sustains you as you wait to see how the pieces fit together?

CHAPTER 51

Our Safe Harbor

There was a time when I was always Melanie's safe place. Her harbor. The place she would run to when troubled. I was always the one she called when there was a concern, a problem, or a question. We were connected, she and I. When she was in trouble I knew before she told me. It didn't matter how easy or difficult the situation, I was the person she counted on and ran to. I was her cheering squad, her defender, her home.

One day, as I sat down to wrap Christmas gifts I came across several holiday bags with Melanie's name on them. There was an automatic catch in my throat as the tears began to gather in my eyes. For a moment as I sat there I began to think about all the holidays we would never share, all the gifts for her that would never fill those pretty bags. I was no longer her safe harbor. My arms were no longer the ones she would run to.

It was then I heard the soft whisper of the Holy Spirit say, "Although you are no longer Melanie's safe harbor, she is in the safest harbor of all. Heaven." Wow! Who better than the Prince of Peace to take care of my girl until we meet again? She's truly home now, in her safe place where there is no fear, no doubt, no sadness, and no feelings of unworthiness.

For me, hope and faith go hand in hand. Despite the pain of grief, we somehow have to find the strength to go on. Hope takes our hand and faith walks along beside us. It's the only way I can manage this journey.

When the waves of grief are hitting hard, faith is my life preserver and hope is the chain attached to it. Hope that I'll see my daughter again one day. Hope that God's promises are true, and he will heal my broken heart. Hope that I am never alone and even when walking through the valley of the shadow of death, he is with me. Hope that joy will come in the morning.

Death is so hard. It takes our loved ones from us where we are no longer able to see them, hold them, or talk with them. But then, God takes their soul. The entire essence of who they are remain with them in heaven. Then thankfully, our mind holds the memories, and nothing can ever take those away from us. We can replay conversations and moments in our mind. Photos bring remembrance of time spent together. And nothing on this earth can ever take away or replace the extraordinary love shared. Then finally...

We can hold tightly to our faith knowing that even as hard as it is to not have them with us today, one day, we will see our loved one again.

Moment of Reflection: God is our safest harbor. We don't have to wait until heaven to find rest there. He offers this peace while we are here on earth.

CHAPTER 52

Grief Like an Earthquake

When Melanie first died my entire being felt on edge. Every movement and sound had an overwhelming intensity to it that was never there before, and my anxiety was at an all-time high and any loud noise would startle me.

Thankfully, as time passed by the anxiety quieted, and my emotions were no longer as explosive as the magnitude of an earthquake. Instead, they became more like the aftershocks. Even today, sudden, or unexpected noises trigger something within me.

One day as I was cooking dinner for my family, my sweet husband approached me from behind. I must have been deep in thought because I didn't hear him. Even something as a gentle kiss on my neck startled me to the point of jumping, while letting out a bit of a cry. Yes, it's the small things that shake me now.

Remembering that Melanie is no longer here with me simmers just below the surface of everything I think or do. As I close my eyes to sleep each night it's the last thing I think of. I wonder if that will ever change? On one hand, I look forward to the day I can drift off to sleep peacefully and not have her death be my last thought. Yet, on the flip side, I'm just as afraid of the day when it happens.

Although some may not equate grief to a catastrophic event, I would beg to differ. Grief feels exactly like an earthquake. It is oftentimes unexpected and comes with its own type of tremors and aftershocks, leaving cracks and gaping holes in our heart.

And just like an earthquake, the effects of grief come in all sizes, and may be different on any given day. Some days it may feel like a 10 on the Richter scale, and other days like a 2. We just never know when it will hit or how hard it will be.

If you don't understand this, be grateful that you don't. It means you've not lost a child or a loved one in an unexpected, traumatic manner. For those who walk this journey alongside me, my heart is joined with yours.

Some say that time heals all wounds, but I don't believe it. What I do believe is when we walk in faith, God continually heals our broken heart. I believe a scar begins to develop over the open wound in our heart and as time goes by the pain may begin to ease. The scar may soften and lighten up, but it will always remain as evidence of what was. We will always know there is a piece of us missing.

The place in our heart which held all the love, hopes and dreams for our loved one can never be filled by anyone or anything else. No amount of time can change that. Yet I will remain confident in the One who has promised to walk alongside me in the valley of the shadow of death. *"Even when I walk through the darkest valley, I will not be afraid, because you are close beside me. Your rod and our staff protect and comfort me" (Psalm 23:4 NLT).*

When the tremors reoccur and the walls threaten to cave in, I remember that the same one also leads me beside the quiet waters and restores my soul. *"He leads me beside quiet waters and refreshes my soul" (Psalm 23:3-4).* This is where my hope during loss comes from. I lean into the only thing I know that will save me from crumbling. His name is Jesus, and my hope will remain in him.

Moment of Reflection: When your world begins to shake like an earthquake where do you draw your hope and strength from?

CHAPTER 53

How Serving Can
Heal the Heart

E ver since I can remember Christmas has always been my favorite holiday. Maybe that's also because it's my birthday as well. My mom always made Christmas very special, and she was certain to keep my birthday celebration separate from the Christmas festivities. It's also not just the day but all the things leading up to it that I love - the lights, the tree, the music, the special recipes shared, getting together with family and friends, and I'll even admit I am one of those who love watching all Hallmark Christmas movies! But do you know what has always been my favorite thing? Deep in my heart I have always loved that I shared the same birthday as Jesus. He is the real reason for this season.

When you're in a state of grief it's hard to conjure up all those feelings of joy, laughter, and excitement. When you begin walking down memory lane, thinking of times past, there is a heightened sense of loss when you know you will never again share it with your loved one.

Our first Christmas without Melanie coincided with the Covid pandemic. It felt like a double whammy to this mother's heart. This meant it would be the first Christmas my daughter would be in heaven, and it also meant it wasn't safe for our son and daughter-in-love to travel to be with us. This would be only the second Christmas in John's lifetime when we would not be together. Instead, we celebrated the way many families did that year, via Zoom!

Although I focused most of my efforts to ensure Cameron had a nice Christmas I shed my share of tears and sadness over Melanie being in heaven. I also decided to remove all expectations for the day and simply do the best I can.

As the weeks drew closer to the actual day I couldn't get away from the stirring in my heart that I wanted, no needed, to do something to remember my girl. So, I chose to honor her memory through giving to other women who faced the same challenges that Melanie did. There are many organizations out there who help support those in recovery, along with those who are still struggling with the disease of addiction.

Melanie had such a big heart and was always giving of the little she had. The day I walked into a women's recovery home with blessing bags for each of them, I was overwhelmed with joy. Although they might have thought I was blessing them, they were each blessing me! It was as if I was loving on Melanie as I looked into the eyes of each one of those women. I shared Melanie's story, hugged them, cried with them, and then prayed with them. It was the best part of my first Christmas without my girl. If you're feeling overwhelmed by the prospect of the holidays without your loved one perhaps you may want to consider doing something in honor of them. It truly does make your heart feel good when you are the hands and feet of Jesus.

When Christmas Day finally arrived, although my heart was still grieving I had no doubt that Melanie was celebrating the birth of Christ unlike anything our minds or heart can fathom. I know she is healed and living in a peace that passes my own understanding. As I learn to focus on her happiness and not my own loss, God continues to comfort my heart in a way that only he can.

Moment of Reflection: By serving others we can honor our loved one and plant positive seeds from our grief.

CHAPTER 54

As the Angelversary Approaches

Every bereaved person I've met along the way has shared with me how stressful and anxiety ridden they become as each angelversary approaches. I think part of that is because we begin to replay each and every minute leading up to the moment we learn of our loved one's death. We also cannot believe that another year is going by without them. In this case, anticipation is not a positive reaction, as we already know the day ahead of us is our worst nightmare, once again, come true.

Other grieving parents have asked me how I am managing to walk this grief journey with such strength. I'm always taken aback by that question because I don't see myself that way. I'm not always strong. Hardly. I take it one moment, one hour, one day at a time, but the main reason I'm able to walk this path is because of my faith. My hope is in God. He is my Rock. My fortress. I ask him to hold my heart in his hands and continue to heal its broken places. I cry out to him daily to give me the peace only he can provide.

When the one-year angelversary arrives, it doesn't mean our grief ends. A parent's grief will never end! It becomes a part of who you are. This message needs to be heard clearly by those who love and support someone walking through the grief journey. Society has somehow decided there is a time limit to grieve. This journey is so very different for everyone.

Some days are better than others, then there are those days which are more like a heavy, wet blanket. What I'm certain of is this - whether I'm up on the mountain top or down in the valley, I'm confident God isn't going to leave me or fail me.

Each year as I approach the date on the calendar that changed the course of this mother's heart I'm going to do my best to chase away the anticipation and anguish of reliving the day my girl went to heaven, and hold on tight to the one who continues to hold me.

Moment of Reflection: We do not find our strength and comfort in man, but in the Lord.

CHAPTER 55

One Year Later: Remembering Melanie

N ever forget. Those two words took on extra meaning for me since Melanie died. It was a day of tragedy and sorrow. It was the day my girl ran ahead to heaven. It's a day which I will never forget.

I'll never forget where I was, what I was doing or who I was with. I remember every single detail of that day.

One of the gifts given to me that day is the knowledge that my Dad was there to guide Melanie safely into the arms of Jesus.

Death is hard and the loss of a child is a loss like no other on this earth. Yet here I am. Still standing, still breathing, and walking this grief journey one day at a time. The tears still flow, and I expect they always will because there will never be a day, I don't miss my girl. The good news is the tears no longer come in the torrential, crashing waves like the tsunami they were in the earlier months, when my heart was so utterly broken. One of God's promises I so tightly held on to is, *"He is close to the brokenhearted and saves those who are crushed in spirit" (Psalm 38:14).* My faith is what continually sustained me and even on those days when I was crawling through the valley, Jesus was right there beside me. He never once left my side. What the enemy meant for evil, God has turned it for His good (Genesis 50:20).

The days of crushing anxiety are fewer and for that I am grateful. Sure, my mind has wandered back to the day I learned of Melanie's death and all the horror that comes with hearing the words no parent should ever hear. There have been times I have relived every moment, over and over again. But now, when I think about Melanie, I choose to look back at how I have been brought through the loss of my only girl.

PEACE: Within the first 24 hours after learning of Melanie's death I felt an overwhelming, powerful, all-encompassing sense of peace that could *only* come from God. There is nothing and no one who can give peace like him. *"And the peace that surpasses all understanding will guard your hearts and minds in Christ Jesus"* *(Phil 4:6 NKJV)*

ENCOURAGEMENT: My Heavenly Father has encouraged and strengthened me in ways that I never felt as strongly as I do now. He delivered His words of love and reassurance deep into my spirit on so many nights through the gift of encouraging songs. *"No one says, 'Where is God my Maker, who gives songs in the night"* *(Job 35:10 NIV)*.

HOPE: Even during that first and darkest night, I never once doubted where my hope and strength would come from. He is my deliverer. My hope. My strength. My rock. My promise keeper. My way maker. *"You keep track of all my sorrows. You have collected all my tears in your bottle. You have recorded each one in your book"* *(Psalm 56:8 NLT)*

Even the saddest experiences we go through in life can become a source of wisdom and strength once we have made peace within our hearts about it. I could write about all the sadness that surrounded the loss of my beautiful girl, but I choose to remember the good. *I choose to remember the love.* The day of her death is not a day I wish to celebrate, but it's a day that has to be acknowledged because it's the day my girl ran ahead to heaven. For me, it was the worst day of my life. For Melanie, it was the best day of hers. I continually strive to reflect on the good that has come from a very tragic situation.

On February 19, 2020 my beautiful girl transitioned to her real home – Heaven. If you too are a believer in Jesus Christ, then you will once again see your loved one. *"He will wipe every tear from their eyes. There will be no more death or mourning or crying or pain, for the old order of things has passed away"(Rev 21:4 NIV).* I take comfort in the fact that I will get to see my daughter again one day. My beautifully broken girl is now totally healed in the presence of his great love.

Looking Through the Lens
Toward Healing and Restoration

L et me begin by saying that I know each one of us is in a different place on our journey. Each of our stories though similar, is also unique. As I continue walking along this path and moving through the grief journey, I learn something new every day. The Lord continues to heal my broken heart and even on those days when I feel the heaviness from missing my girl, I run to my Heavenly Father.

I'm discovering when you suffer a loss and the grief is so deep, healing and restoration can seem so far off and unattainable. Walking through the early days, weeks, and months of grief I found it was hard to concentrate on much. Sometimes the only thing I could focus on was breathing – literally one breath at a time.

However, I do believe in healing and restoration. I believe when you lose a loved one you begin to think differently. I know for me my eyes are more focused on heaven and the life after this. As a believer in Christ, I have always known this is not our home, yet it never became more alive to me until Melanie died. When my only daughter's home became heaven the lens through which I viewed things became very different. It pulled my thoughts away from superficial things and took my mind behind the veil. I also found it removed me from my own comfortable little bubble and made me laser focused on more important things in life.

God is a god of healing and deliverance. Is it easy? Not always. Will it take time? Definitely. I didn't wake up one day with my heart totally healed and restored. He's still restoring me piece by piece, day by day.

As I've been thinking about healing and restoration it reminded me of a time about 20 years ago when my mother-in-law gifted my husband and me with two antique pieces of furniture which have been in his family for over 130 years. We were in the middle of building a new house and my mother-in-law wanted so much for us to have these pieces to add to our new home. It was such a sweet and generous gesture, and while we didn't want to disappoint her, when we saw the condition they were in we couldn't imagine them in our brand-new home. Each piece had beautiful stained, leaded glass in the shape of intricate diamonds on the doors, however, they hadn't been properly cared for in many years and the wood had a heavy layer of what appeared as dark black lacquer. Not wanting to offend her we took the pieces home and put them in the garage. After several weeks and many hours of research we decided to try and restore the pieces ourselves. As we tackled the first piece, we spent every waking hour, every weekend for several weeks with steel wool in hand, cleaning, stripping, and scrubbing repeatedly. Slowly, we began to remove the black layer that had accumulated over the years of neglect. Around the fourth week into the project, and just about the time I was ready to give up, I began to see some light shining through from the heavy darkness on the buffet. I started getting a little excited as I saw the beauty beneath the surface. Below the thick black covering was a tiger oak wood in beautiful condition. This gave me the incentive I needed to continue scrubbing and sanding. Although the project wasn't easy and took months of our time and energy the result made it was so worthwhile. If we can take a piece of furniture that was so dark and ugly and turn it into a thing of beauty, it makes me think of what God can do for us, his children. It reminds me of the verse of scripture in Isaiah 61:3 where God "gives beauty for ashes."

I realize these are inanimate objects which mean nothing to God, but just like the beauty that was hidden under the surface of the dark, black wood it is the same with our Heavenly Father. He longs to remove the heavy darkness that has settled over our broken hearts and wants to bring restoration and healing to us. I miss my daughter so very much, but I've never doubted for a moment that she wouldn't want me to remain submerged in depression and despair over her death.

After the loss of a loved one, it's easy for our hearts to become so dark like the pieces of furniture which were not properly cared for. If you yearn for your heart to be healed, the first step in doing so is just to ask him. Jesus is a gentleman and will not barge into your life uninvited. Simply invite Him in and ask Him to heal your hurting heart and begin to restore your joy.

"Are you weary, carrying a heavy burden? Then come to me. I will refresh your life, for I am your oasis. Simply join your life with mine. Learn my ways and you'll discover that I'm gentle, humble, easy to please. You will find refreshment and rest in me. For all that I require of you will be pleasant and easy to bear" (Matthew 11:28-30 TPT).

As I continue this grief journey, I am confident there is hope after loss. It's not an instantaneous restoration, but a gradual healing – at least that's how it's been for me. Some days I take a few stumbling steps backward, but I continue to look heavenward, to the place where my girl is and know when it's my time to go, that's the place I long to be.

ACKNOWLEDGMENTS

Thank you, Jesus for walking beside me every step along the way of this grief journey, and for carrying me when I didn't think I could take another step. May sharing this story bring light and love into the dark, lonely places and allow others to see with you by our side, there truly is, Hope During Loss.

Thank you to my husband, Fred, my life partner, and my strong tower every day but especially during the darkest of storms. Our Heavenly Father knew exactly what I needed when he brought you into my life. Thank you for being a Godly example of a man, a husband, and a father to our children.

Thank you to my son, John, the first one who made me a mom and who I love more than these words will ever convey. The greatest gift God ever gave me was the gift of being your mother. You have always inspired me to be my best, and I love how God has infused you with such love, and strength. You have a depth and sensitivity that is both rare and precious.

Cameron, my incredibly amazing son who God blessed me with when I least expected it. I am so honored to be your mom. Even at this young age you have a gift of discernment. You would often walk into the room and with only a look and no words being exchanged you would know I was having a moment of missing our Melanie and would immediately come wrap your arms around me offering love and comfort. God has a special plan for your life, and I can't wait to see it unfold.

Anna Mitchael, thank you for being the best Editor a first-time author could ask for. I'm so grateful for your guidance, encouragement, and direction as you helped me breathe life into *Beautifully Broken* in an honest, transparent, and vulnerable way.

This story would never have been brought to life without the help, support, and love of so many others who provided support along the journey. Everyone deserves to have friends who are like family and God has blessed me with a small group of women who have been there for me whether in the valley or on the mountain top.

Patty M., my lifelong friend and sister of the heart. There isn't a moment in my life where you have not been weaved into the major pieces of the tapestry of my life. You've walked every step hand-in-hand with me. Thank you for being that constant source of love and support.

Rosalind, my dearest friend since grade school, you have been a friend like no other. You have been on this journey with me since the beginning. My admiration, and gratitude for you is endless. You are grace under pressure and your love and care knows no bounds.

Joyce, whether near or far you are such a source of strength. Our long Saturday morning coffee chats have sustained me more than you know. It's so comforting to have a friend who sticks closer than a brother, or in this case a sister. I am so grateful for you.

Kathleen, thank you for being my constant prayer partner and warrior for Christ. Thank you for praying for my girl for all those years – it was not in vain. Those prayers probably saved her life on more times than we know.

Patty F., Diane, Michele, Cynthia, and Doreen, you have all been the wind beneath my wings. Each one of you has unselfishly been there for me, even from afar. You've brought love, light, care, and encouragement and many hours of lending me your ears and shoulders. I love each of you and appreciate you so very much.

Thank you to my friend, Margaret, who was my second set of eyes when the pages began to blur together.

Thank you to my brother and sister for all your support, and to my nieces who loved Melanie like a sister. Much love to you all.

Finally, to all the others who have lifted up my arms and heart when I was weary, thank you! To all the grieving hearts, may you find encouragement within these pages, and know that you are never truly alone.

"My flesh and my heart may fail, but God is the strength of my heart and my portion forever" Psalm 73:26